THE FOWL OF THE AIR,

THE FISH OF THE SEA

and the

BEASTS OF THE FIELD

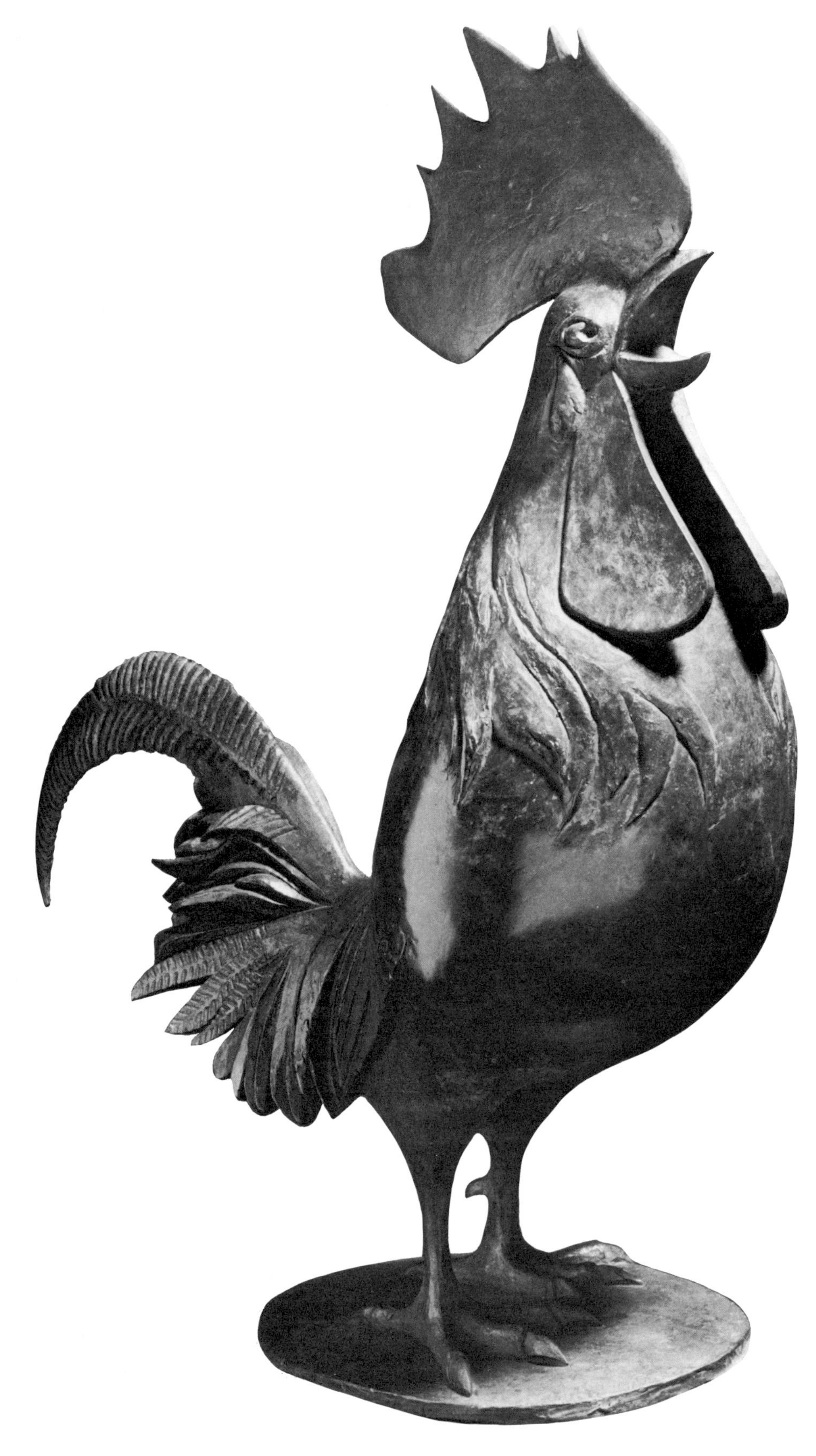

THE FOWL OF THE AIR, THE FISH OF THE SEA, & THE BEASTS OF THE FIELD:

the animal sculptures of ELLIOT OFFNER

MUSEUM OF FINE ARTS
SPRINGFIELD, MASSACHUSETTS
SEPTEMBER 23 – NOVEMBER 4

FORUM GALLERY
NEW YORK, NEW YORK
NOVEMBER 10 – 30
MCMLXXXIV

MUSEUM OF FINE ARTS
SPRINGFIELD, MASSACHUSETTS

1 9 8 4

MUSEUM OF FINE ARTS, SPRINGFIELD, MASSACHUSETTS

Director: Richard Mühlberger
Curator of American Art: Martha J. Hoppin
Assistant Curator / Exhibitions: Steven Kern
Registrar: Karen Papineau
Assistant Registrar: Nancy L. Swallow
Preparator: Melvin Wachowiak
Editor: Debra Gorlin
Photographer: David Stansbury

The operation of the Museum of Fine Arts and all of its programs is made possible with support from the Massachusetts Council on the Arts and Humanities, a state agency, and the Institute of Museum Services, a Federal agency.

Photographic Credits: Front Cover & Frontispiece, David Stansbury
Back Cover, E. Irving Blomstrann

Photograph Credits: 1, 2, 3, Hyman Edelstein, Northampton; 4, Walter Russell, N.Y.; 5, 9, Wendy Snyder McNeil, Cambridge, Mass.; 6, 8, 10, Peter Johnson, New Haven, Conn.; 7, 19, 22, 25, 27, 29, 30, David Stansbury, Springfield, Mass.; 12, Stephen Petegorsky, Northampton, Mass.; 12, 13, 15, 16, 17, 20, 21, 26, George Dimock, Easthampton, Mass.; 23, 24, E. Irving Blomstrann, New Britain, Conn.; 28, Elliot Offner; Text Frontispiece, Gabriel Amadeus Cooney, Whately, Mass.

International Standard Book Number: 0–916746–08–9
Library of Congress Catalog Card Number: 84–51619
© 1984 Springfield Library and Museums Association
for the Museum of Fine Arts, Springfield, Massachusetts

LENDERS TO THE EXHIBITION

Mr. and Mrs. Manuel Baker
Deerfield Academy
Mr. and Mrs. Marvin Flowerman
Dr. and Mrs. Michael Hume
Dr. and Mrs. Kristaps J. Keggi
Museum of Fine Arts, Springfield, Massachusetts
Rosemary O'Connell Offner
Private Collector

TABLE OF CONTENTS

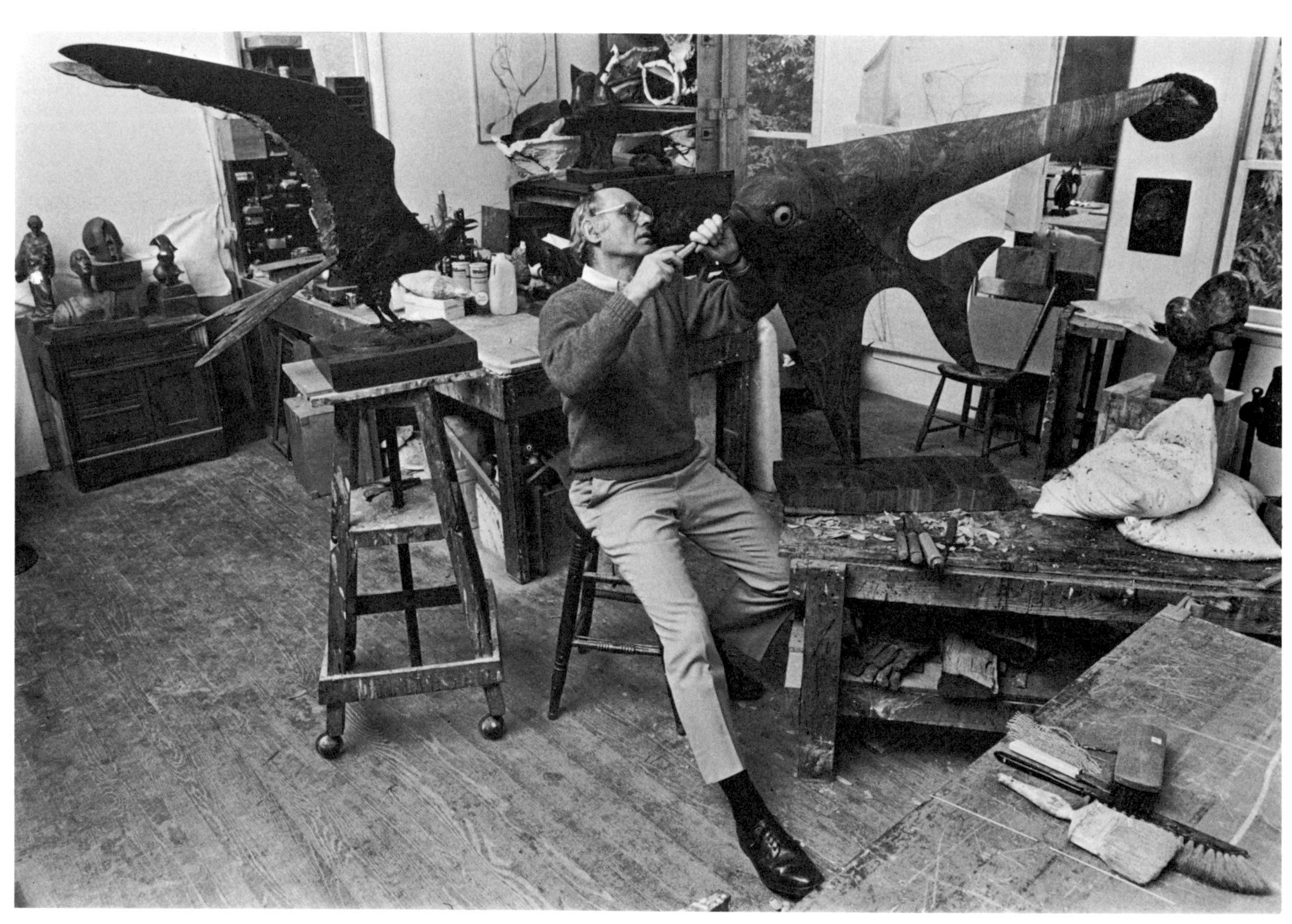

MANY of the features which characterize Elliot Offner's sculpture were established very early in his career. The study of natural form, a reverence for art of the past, and a love of drawing have been constant forces shaping his work. As an artist committed to working in the figurative tradition, he has remained tied to subject matter, especially to human and animal figures.

"I never seriously entertained doing anything but art," Offner recalled from his child-hood.★ Encouraged by his mother to draw at a young age, he had some art instruction in elementary school and took art courses in high school in Brooklyn, where he grew up in the 1940's. He considers these courses of little significance compared with those experiments he carried out on his own—drawing often at the Brooklyn Botanic Garden, sketching old houses in his neighborhood, and doing pen and ink studies from nature. To satisfy his curiosity about art, he frequently went to The Brooklyn Musem where he was particularly attracted to the Egyptian art collection. When he was young, his interest in art included architecture and archaeology, two fields which he thought he might enter someday.

Upon graduation from high school, Offner attended Cooper Union in New York City from 1949 to 1952. He chose Cooper Union because there, unlike the course of study offered at other art institutions, he could pursue architecture, which he studied for two years, as well as painting. At this time his attraction to three-dimensional objects was directed toward architecture rather than sculpture. However, painting became his chief concern, although he continued to draw. He also developed a new interest in calligraphy through contact with George Salter and Paul Standard, both on the Cooper Union faculty.

While Offner studied painting at Cooper Union with Morris Kantor and John Ferren, he maintains that the important influences came indirectly in these years, and that no one outstanding teacher directed him. Probably most important as indirect influences were the approach of calligrapher Paul Standard and the fine decorative art, print, and book collec-tion of the Cooper-Hewitt Museum, then housed in Cooper Union. Using this collection Offner taught himself a great deal about the history of graphic art. William Morris' books, for example, were a revelation to him. As before, he frequented New York museums, feeling that Cooper Union's teachers and curriculum placed too little emphasis on the study of past art.

After finishing Cooper Union, Offner went on to study with Josef Albers at Yale, where he completed his BFA in 1953. He remembers this experience as an important influence on his career, even though his later work does not directly show Albers' impact. Excited by

★All the information presented here was drawn from interviews with Elliot Offner in June 1984.

Albers' "beliefs, ideas, and devotion to art as a way of life," Offner concentrated on color studies and painting. Until this point, as he describes it, Offner had been working to improve the skills of drawing and painting, while generating his own ideas and subjects. New ideas now came from Albers, who was a dynamic, stimulating teacher. Offner even had a chance to work on a cooperative architectural project under Buckminster Fuller. At Yale, Offner also drew at the Peabody Museum of Natural History, as he had done earlier at the Brooklyn Botanic Garden, and he furthered his knowledge of books and printing through the Sterling Library collections.

Offner's study at Yale was interrupted for four years. From 1953 to 1955, serving in the United States Army, he was stationed in the American south and midwest, where he found every opportunity to visit whatever museum and historical society he could find. He was enthusiastic about the Oriental art collection at The Nelson-Atkins Museum of Art in Kansas City, Missouri and compelled by the strong narrative aspect of their collection of American nineteenth-century genre painting. The emphasis on subject matter in these American works countered the strongly formal approach of Albers.

In 1955 Offner took a job as calligrapher and designer for Steuben Glass in New York City, and less than two years later he married Rosemary O'Connell, a woman of great intelligence and understanding who has been his partner in all things since then. While he seriously considered remaining with Steuben, he "had the realization that I was either going to be a serious artist or I was not." Encouraged by his wife he went to consult Albers, whose response was, "Well, Offner, of course you can come back." He returned to New Haven with Rosemary in 1957, where he remained for two years, and where the first of their three children was born.

By now, however, Offner believed that his ideas would be best expressed in sculpture and began to work three-dimensionally, preferring "the glories of clear, tangible but complex form" to the illusionary form of painting. About Offner's new direction, Albers commented, "Boy, if the wind is blowing that way, go with the wind." During this year of his return to Yale, Offner worked mostly on his own, experimenting with sculptural forms, mainly geometric constructions, often with architectural character.

For Offner, these Yale years were exciting but tumultuous for additional reasons. During his second year, he felt torn between his loyalty to the retiring Albers and his admiration of the newly appointed Rico Lebrun, whose figurative, expressionistic work contrasted sharply with Albers' objective, abstract style. Offner regards Lebrun as a seminal influence on his work and considers this year as a critical period in his life. Lebrun gave Offner fresh ideas for his sculpture, as well as the impetus for him to return to representational subject matter. In this revelatory period, Offner began to see how his own artistic concerns interrelated; he found connections between his past activities, his present enthusiasms, and those artists whom he revered.

This special synthesis of Offner's interests as an artist was to take several years to be fully realized in his sculpture. After graduating from Yale in 1959 with an MFA degree, he worked briefly for The City Printing Co. in New Haven as a typographic designer to support his family. Beginning that fall, he taught for one year in the Art Department of the University of Massachusetts in Amherst. The next year, 1960, he accepted a teaching position in the Art Department at Smith College in nearby Northampton. In 1975 Smith honored Offner's work as artist and teacher by naming him the Andrew W. Mellon Professor in the Humanities, a chair which he continues to hold.

Between 1961 and 1965, Offner was making many sculptures of female figures that often recalled themes from the Old Testament. During this time, however, he also undertook a major sculptural project about which he had been thinking for years. It was a memorial to the Holocaust which would consist of three life-size figures, wrought in plaster, to be cast in bronze. There were also many other smaller studies in bronze in the round and in relief, as well as a life-size wood carving. The Holocaust series incorporated some of his discoveries at Yale while bringing together a number of threads from his past. Both of his parents were Jews who fled from Austria and Poland to America at the time of World War I. Before and after World War II, members of his family who survived the Nazi persecutions arrived at the Offner home in Brooklyn, bringing tales of death, horror, and miraculous survival. The memories of those terrible events and personal tragedy were always in the forefront of his consciousness, and it was inevitable that he would speak of these thoughts to Rico Lebrun when they met in 1958. Since his youth, Offner had wanted to find a way to give form to these deep emotional experiences but did not know how to go about it. He was encouraged by Lebrun to attempt the subject. While at Yale, Offner had helped to hang an exhibition of Lebrun's work which included a series of massive, recent drawings and paintings of the Holocaust, showing distorted and dismembered bodies. Offner was impressed with the power of these works.

An important catalyst in Offner's interpretation of the Holocaust was his first-hand exposure to medieval sculpture during his initial trip to Europe in 1961. The Offners journeyed to many great Romanesque and Gothic architectural sites on the continent. Offner admits to being more interested in the Romanesque, which would always continue to affect his sculpture in various subtle forms. A large photograph of the sculpture of Eve carved by the great master of Autun, Gislebertus, sits above his desk, where he looks at it each day. Still, it was the "Gothic woodcarvers of France, Germany and the Netherlands, who," he has said, "in their special way, made some of the greatest works of art in history which successfully depicted the agony of man." They provided an example, for which he had been searching, of art whose meaning was both specific and transcendent. He began to see in the martyred figures of the victims of Auschwitz and Buchenwald resemblance in form and content to the agonized images of the Gothic Pietas and Crucifixions. The skeletal, twisted, single figures of Offner's sculptures strongly recall the Gothic imagery, while unmistakably retaining their own identity as figures of the concentration camps. While the bronzes were conceived as a group of three, nearly all the sculptures have become separated in private and public collections. One of the studies is in the Hirshhorn Museum and Sculpture Garden, and two of the life-size bronzes are in The Brooklyn Museum and the Cathedral of St. John the Divine in New York City, respectively.

In working these sculptures, Offner studied photographs in Amsterdam of the War, made and consulted photographs of Gothic sculpture, and made careful drawings of anatomical structure, particularly of bones. He has used these methods of working in his later sculptures as well. This combination of drawing from nature and studying artistic precedents links Offner to the approach of artists from the Renaissance through the nineteenth century. That he would seek to learn from great art places him within a traditional framework. Artists whom he speaks of with ease and admiration include Donatello, Hans Brüggemann, Tilman Riemenschneider, Auguste Rodin, Constantin Brancusi, Constantin Meunier, and Georges Minne, to mention only a few. "I never stop trying to learn more about those sculptors whose work constitutes our heritage and enriches our civilization. The more I learn, the better my work can be," he says.

Offner's sculptural career can be divided into three phases. The first occurred between 1958 and 1964, when he made many works which relate to his background, such as the Holocaust subjects, and the matriarchal structure of his family. Some of his most successful sculptures from these years are of large-proportioned women whom he viewed as heroic. These small bronzes and larger wood carvings, according to Offner, reflect in part figures of a certain kind of European matriarchy and the dominant role his mother and grandmother played in his life. At the same time these figures also depicted female characters from the Old Testament, such as *Woman of the Exodus* (Joe & Emily Lowe Art Gallery, Syracuse University). In form, they bear some similarity to works by artists whom he respects: Gaston Lachaise, Ernst Barlach, and Aristide Maillol.

In this period, Offner formed an important friendship with sculptor and printmaker Leonard Baskin, who was also teaching at Smith College. Offner recalls that through their long conversations, he learned as much from Baskin as he did from any other artist. He speaks of Baskin as a learned and most generous man, who shared his knowledge willingly and helped younger artists. Not surprisingly, Offner's work shared similarities with that of Baskin's. Both sculptors carved wood, depicted the human figure, executed Biblical subjects, and maintained a humanist outlook.

Offner has almost always worked in both wood and bronze. Initially, he took more interest in wood carving, benefitting from the direct carving movement of the 1930's in America. Yet, because the realization of his ideas in wood involved a lengthy process, he began working in bronze, executing his first cast pieces about 1962, helped by a grant from Smith College.

Offner's sculpture has always been profoundly affected by his personal response to world events, as the Holocaust figures amply demonstrate. During the second phase of his career, from 1965 to 1971, the form and content of his sculpture expressed his emotional anguish over the Vietnam War. He no longer represented the female form, nor the distorted, disfigured bodies of the Holocaust series. Instead, he sculptured single heads, enshrouded or helmeted, passive and mute. Reading about the Crusades, he saw parallels between them and current events, often using the names of medieval leaders of campaigns as the titles for some of his own sculptures. Toward the end of this period he began to work with themes of metamorphosis, continuing to express these ideas through the form of the single or multiple, joined heads. Surfaces were occasionally embellished with pattern work not unlike the decorative forms in Celtic and Romanesque art. Also manifest in these sculptures was Offner's understanding of anatomical structure as well as a feeling for form shaped by the armorer's craft.

A turning point in Offner's career came in 1970 during a sabbatical year in England, when he slowly disengaged himself from the art work which he had done as a response to the Vietnam War. Even while he was completing a complex series of multiple-headed sculptures of a mysterious and complex psychological character (three-headed maquette [fig. 7]), he began to make drawings in the British Museum of Natural History, returning to familiar methods of working stemming from his earliest days as an artist. From this experience came a new direction in his sculpture and inaugurated the third and current phase of his career. Offner's drawings of fish fossils were the start of a continually expanding interest in animal sculpture which has come to be the dominant theme in his sculptures.

Offner's first animal sculptures were reliefs based on his drawings of fish fossils, which in reality are almost flat, as are Offner's drawings of them. His relief sculpture is thus an imaginative recreation of fish remains. These earliest works, such as *Dapedium Granulatum*, 1971 (fig. 1) are bronzes with a rich surface texture. Although he had previously done only five or six relief sculptures, he had carefully studied the works of masters such as Donatello, Giovanni della Robbia, and Augustus St. Gaudens. In 1981 Offner executed the largest relief he has done, a portrait of Karl Lehmann with a carved English and Greek inscription commemorating Dr. Lehmann's work as Director of the American Archaeological Expedition to Samothrace, Greece. The plaque is on the façade of the Museum in Samothrace.

At the same time that Offner was exploring animals as subject matter for his sculpture, he pursued other themes as well. The catalogue listing for Offner's 1972 exhibition at the Forum Gallery reveals that the preponderance of sculptures shown were the single- and multiple-headed images of brooding but classic countenance. Along with these were two 1971 sculptures of Gregory the Great, a medieval religious figure of wide accomplishment and historical importance for whom there were only a few outstanding artistic representations. Offner began to focus some of his attention upon Gregory and then upon other historical personages whom he admired and whom he judged could be fit subjects for his thought and sculpture. Last year he finished a woodcut and a relief sculpture of Sir Thomas More.

Perhaps more important as signal works for a new emphasis in the content of his sculpture were four fish reliefs, shown along with the butternut *Fish* of 1972, his first animal sculpture in the round (fig. 4). In 1975, Offner carved another large work, a *Hatchet Fish* (fig. 10) and this year he completed what he regards as the best of these sculptures, *Angel Fish* (fig. 29 & front cover), which incorporates a sense of motion quite unlike any of the previous sculptures. Two other fish are of bronze and were executed as studies for the larger wood carvings.

While working on his fish sculptures about 1973, Offner made some sculptures of animal skulls in both bronze and wood. This particular subject matter was familiar, as he had made skull studies for his Holocaust figures as well as using skull forms in several of the multiple heads. In these new sculptures Offner used his long-standing approach to the figure, seeing it in terms of its underlying structure: "One way I have always studied form is to study the remarkable complexity and beauty of the curvature of bones," he says. These animal skull works began with drawings made from small skulls found in the woods. The two bronzes are about three times actual size, while the large maple wood carving (fig. 8) is perhaps thirteen times the size of the actual skull, which was probably from a bird. Offner feels that by greatly changing the scale, and in setting the object on its back end, the image becomes transfigured into a form still beautiful but easily seen as something other than a skull. He believes these works are related to the fish and bird sculptures because they are part of his general return to natural forms after 1970.

The greatest number of fully three-dimensional animal sculptures have been representations of birds. The first of these was a *Mythical Bird*, which he finished carving in birch in early 1976 (fig. 13). The next year Offner was completely occupied with the execution of a life-size wood carving of St. Francis of Assisi. This commission was an outgrowth of the 1975 International Exhibition of Liturgical Art associated with the Eucharistic Congress held that year in Philadelphia, in which benefactors sought to give church commissions to leading American artists.

The St. Francis proved a challenge since the saint had been interpreted by such geniuses as Donatello, Giovanni Bellini, and Giotto, among others. After much thought and study, Offner concluded that the only model he could think of who possessed the kind of innocence needed to portray the spirit of St. Francis was a child. His fifteen-year-old son posed for the sculpture. Two maquettes for that work are in this exhibition (figs. 11, 12). The St. Francis wood carving was shown at a major Offner exhibition in the spring and summer of 1977 at the Smith College Museum of Art, after which the Offners left to live another year in England, with travel to the continent.

Abroad once more, Offner began to concentrate again on the animal sculptures, with particular emphasis on birds. At the same time he continued to make drawings, take photographs of landscapes, continually look at art, and store up visual information which would "affect my thought and work in its own mysterious ways."

Despite the interruptions of commissioned work, the fish and bird sculptures, as well as his earlier sculpture of the 1960's, demonstrate that Offner has tended to work in a series, exploring nuances of form and surface in his variations on a theme. In the animal sculptures he usually tried to approximate reality, so that the type of bird or fish would be very recognizable, though not a direct copy or reproduction of reality. He simplified surface detail, contrasting isolated sections of decorative pattern with smooth surfaces and contours, and emphasized repeating curves of form which create graceful and powerful silhouettes.

To inspire him in the creation of his animal sculptures, Offner consulted a variety of sources, including the art of the past. Greatly moved by the Romanesque sculpture at

Autun, Vezelay and other sites since his first trip to Europe in 1961, he continues to be impressed by the animals carved on capitals and portals, as well as the simplified form of modelling employed for them. He also admires the representations of animals by ancient sculptors, especially Assyrian reliefs, whose simplified contours, decorative patterns, and rounded forms bear a transfigured resemblance to his sculptures. Among more recent art, he studied animal sculpture by John Flanagan, Elie Nadelman, Gaston Lachaise, and particularly by American folk artists of the nineteenth century. For his animal sculpture Offner continued to draw from life, to study illustrations in natural history books, and to read about animals. The model for his *Hatchet Fish* of 1975 (fig. 10) was a prosaic dead fish about one inch long from his young son's fish tank.

In addition to the sculpture, Offner has executed prints of animal subjects since 1974. Since he had always maintained a strong interest in the graphic arts, most notably the area of letter form, fine printing and typography (he is Printer to the College at Smith, and he and Rosemary have a private press), it was natural for him to take up printmaking and to work exclusively in the medium of woodcut. While his sculpture has been principally of birds and fish, his prints represent a wider variety of animals, including the lion, giraffe, and boar. Sometimes the prints serve as a point of departure for an idea that is then carried out in sculpture. For example, the *Lion of Judah* woodcut of 1974 was followed by a small bronze in 1976 (fig. 15) and a large wood sculpture in 1979 (fig. 21). The large bronze turkey, Offner's most recent work, had its origins as a print as well. The idea for this subject had been in the artist's mind for years. He saw Giovanni Bologna's *Turkey* in the Bargello in 1961, and he has kept a small postcard of it on his studio wall since then, thinking that he would make his own interpretation of a turkey one day. It was not until 1982 that Offner made the woodcut, while the bronze *Turkey* of 1984 (fig. 30) was the last work completed for this exhibition.

Over the years, much of Offner's sculpture has given expression to the human suffering caused by the grave political crises of the 20th century. In 1966, The National Institute of Arts and Letters gave him an award and published the following citation in their *Proceedings*: "With compelling form and unequivocal voice Elliot Offner has taken his place as one of the most ardent spokesmen for that concern with the human condition which is still making legitimate claims on twentieth-century sculpture." In his recent work, however, he has chosen to convey another side of the human condition. With loving objectivity, he has created animal sculptures which celebrate the serenity and harmony of the natural world.

Martha J. Hoppin, *Curator of American Art*
Museum of Fine Arts
Springfield, Massachusetts

FOR the title of this exhibition of his animal sculptures, Elliot Offner chose the phrase, "the fowl of the air, the fish of the sea, the beasts of the field," which comes from the creation story in the first and second chapters of the *Book of Genesis*. The Old Testament writer tells us that on the fifth day of creation, the waters of the earth were populated with fish; and in the open firmament above, with fowl that fly; and on the sixth day, "out of the ground the Lord God formed every beast of the field." That same day, God created man "in His own image." Though the precise meaning of the phrase, "in His own image," has been the subject of debate and speculation by scholars and holy men for centuries, yet, in the context of an art exhibition, it seems so clear that one of the divine attributes that the Maker passed on to humankind was the gift of creation itself.

If one literally interprets those words of *Genesis*, "formed out of the ground," then quite plausibly the Creator can be considered the first sculptor, who made his creatures out of clay, and other materials of the earth to form the likenesses of animals. Although these sculptors have not literally breathed the "breath of life" into their own forms, the best of them have produced images that evoke the very life and dynamism of their animal models.

In the traditions of Western art, animals—with their potential for decorative effects and symbolic associations—have fascinated artists since the beginning of human history, when the first paintings were made on cave walls. During the 11th and 12th centuries, animals appear regularly in tapestries and in the margins of illuminated manuscripts, depicted with greater fidelity to nature than ever before in art. By the 15th century, animals perch, prance, roam, fly, and even fight, in the backgrounds of paintings, and by the 16th century, they finally take center stage.

The animal as a significant subject matter gained some prominence in Western art in the studios of Raphael (Italian, 1483–1520) and Rubens (Flemish, 1577–1640). Both of these masters relied upon specialists to accurately paint animals in their compositions, and to place them in the foreground, where they would give veracity to the settings, and act as a foil to the quirks and foibles of man.

For his famous tapestry cartoon, *The Miraculous Draught of Fishes*, c. 1515, Raphael called on the expertise of Giovanni da Udine to paint the fishes in the boat, the ravens wheeling overhead, and the cranes along the shore. Raphael based his cartoon on the story from the New Testament in which Jesus instructs his disciples, who have been fishing fruitlessly all night, to cast their net on the other side of the boat. The artist pictures them at that point in the narrative when, at long last, they laboriously but successfully haul in the catch.

Standing in the foreground of the tapestry, the cranes, which like the disciples, have been frustrated in their attempts to fish, appear to be a kind of Greek chorus, engaged in a commentary on this astonishing event taking place before them. They seem to be exclaiming, "Why didn't we think of that?" Though Raphael must be credited for his brilliant dramatization of the story, Udine, who was familiar with the plumage, anatomy, and habits of the cranes, provides it with the necessary credibility. His naturalistic depiction of the animals balances Raphael's imaginative treatment of the disciples, whose exaggerated musculature gives them the appearance of supermen. Also, the presence of the cranes, shorebirds found in eastern and southern regions of the Mediterranean, authenticate the setting. Raphael's cartoon is an isolated, albeit powerful example, of the representation of animals in a work of art in the early 16th century.

It was not until the late 16th century that the subject was taken up again. For those artists in the circles of Peter Paul Rubens and Jan Brueghel the Elder, animals became not only a significant, but a customary, subject matter. Animals also figured as central *dramatis personae* in the proverbs and fables that were of great interest to the Northern painters at the end of the 16th and the beginning of the 17th centuries. One of these artists, Frans Snyders', a collaborator of Rubens, populated his paintings with animals of all sorts. He seems to have been the first artist to isolate animals from their natural setting and to present them as the sole subject of a work of art. Snyders' paintings of this kind bear dates of around 1615 to the 1630's.

The generations of Dutch artists from the 1650's through the century became the first to specialize exclusively in animal subjects. By the start of the 18th century, this genre had spread throughout the rest of Europe. From the age of Rubens and Brueghel through the first half of the 18th century the most distinguished artists of this genre possessed an expertise as much in the psychology of animals and their interactions with one another and their habitat, as in their anatomy and markings.

By the late 18th century, painters of this specialty had lost touch with their animal subjects, producing hackneyed copies of the brilliant compositions and ideas of the earlier masters. For sculptors, however, the subject of animals engendered a new school of art. Known as the *animaliers*, these sculptors made bronzes of groups of animals, as well as of individual animals, representing them in highly naturalistic ways. Although the origins of this genre of sculpture go back to the 16th century and even earlier, the most famous of the *animaliers* was Antoine Barye (French, 1796–1875), whose work is represented in the permanent collection of the Museum of Fine Arts. Although Offner's work is neither influenced stylistically by the *animaliers*, nor by their predecessors, the great animal painters of the 17th and 18th centuries, his animal sculptures belong to the same tradition inasmuch as they remain true to the animals' real life surroundings. But whereas the French sculptors often hint at the environment in their works, including a tuft of grass here, or a branch there, Offner supplies no such concrete traces of the animals' habitats. His animals are totally removed from the forest, field, or pond; however, they behave as though they were still there. They seem to be responding to their natural surroundings with that precarious intelligence that either enables them to survive or causes them to perish.

Using slight asymmetry, Offner is able to recreate the clumsy gait of a turkey (fig. 30), or to capture the stretch of the neck and gentle turn of the head of a pheasant in a posture of defensive alertness. In showing its round eye opened wide, he portrays the bittern's vulnerability and secretiveness, while the raptorial crouch of the kite dramatically evokes its swift aggressiveness. These subtleties of expression and stance suggest a natural setting. The turkey proudly plods across a field; the pheasant listens closely to the sound of a potential predator hidden in the brush. In his upright stretch the bittern imitates the reeds that surround him, uncertain that he has escaped notice. Just alighting near its nest, the kite calls out against an intruder. In these sculptures, the natural world, though invisible, is all there, as if Offner had painted a grand canvas.

Even those sculptural elements which appear at first to be purely decorative devices, such as the round beading across the side of a large wooden fish (fig. 29 & front cover), ultimately function as signs of the environment. The beads become bubbles of air, rising to the surface of a lagoon, as the fish turns elegantly but abruptly, fleeing a pursuer, or chasing its mate. From an anatomical point of view, the beads correspond to those points where the fish's ribs are closest to its skin. For this sculpture, Offner studied a dead fish from his son's aquarium to achieve this balance between anatomy and decoration, illusion and reality.

While walking in the woods, the artist found the diminutive skull of a bird, and another time, the skull of a small nocturnal animal. He took them home with him and they became the models for the two bronze skulls in this exhibition (figs. 5, 6). Experimenting with several sculptural versions of these skulls, Offner enlarged them several times their original size. Fascinated by these enlargements, he decided to magnify his representation of the bird skull to its furthest limit, without knowing how this would affect its identity as a recognizable form. The result was his carved maple sculpture, *Great Wood Skull* (fig. 8). In this work, the small bird skull has been transfigured into a gigantic, abstract form, sleek, sensuous, and richly warm, yet still a remarkably accurate if larger version of the original bony model. Offner's intentions were not scientific at all, but entirely artistic. He met the most essential and rudimentary obligations of the artist: to find, identify, and observe natural beauty in the world outside him, and to create from the true vision that is within. His impulse to create new forms is evident when Offner combines the same bird skull with the skull of a human being in *Heads & Skull in Metamorphosis* (fig. 7).

Offner's sculptures evolve equally from his careful studies of art as from his scrutiny of animal behavior. Some pieces, in fact, owe more to art than to nature. The artist, for instance, could not make his *Lion of Judah* (fig. 21) into a fierce beast, or even a convincingly feline one. Though he attempted such an interpretation, the intellectual sources for his depiction of the lion overpowered the naturalistic references. In Offner's view, the lion is more an iconic than a real animal, akin to the small but monumental Celtic-inspired symbols of Saint Mark in the illuminated manuscripts of the 8th century, or to Romanesque lions like the one dating from 1166 in the Cathedral Square in Braunschweig. The conventions, which

Offner employs to represent the *Lion of Judah* as a symbol of state, religion, and history, give it a timeless presence.

The depth of Offner's knowledge and respect for tradition which is so apparent in the *Lion of Judah* can also be assayed in his use of calligraphy. He regularly uses the 16th-century Chancery Cursive script, of which he is one of the great contemporary masters, in carved signatures of his works. But, in so doing, he does not so much pay obeisance to the past as he does to the qualities of elegance and grace, which characterize all of his works, whether rich in historical symbolism or not.

Offner has no compunctions about using animals to symbolize ideas which are otherwise quite removed from their animal nature. Although he altered the form of a lion to recall the rich and powerful heritage of the *Lion of Judah* he has also used animals as symbols far more prosaically. In 1981 he was commissioned to execute a public monument to stand near the corner of Willow and Cross Streets at the end of a small pedestrian park that links Armory Commons with Main Street in downtown Springfield, Massachusetts. He chose the crowing cockerel as his subject. Entitled *Awakening*, the bronze bird, a similar cast of which is in this exhibition (frontispiece), stands atop an eight-foot plinth. Its lordly stride and erect comb speak of confidence and dominion. Its morning cry is symbolic of the reawakening and revitalization of the district over which it presides, where abandoned factories have been transformed into stylish apartment dwellings. A preparatory drawing of the subject is in the permanent collection of the Museum of Fine Arts.

One sculpture of a human figure has been included in this exhibition, *Saint Francis as a Youth* (fig. 11), for whom Offner's son, Daniel, posed as the model. A larger version is housed at the St. Charles Seminary in Overbrook, Pennsylvania. The artist shows the saint with a bird in his hand, a reminder that Francis once preached to these creatures. His sermon could be seen as an act of a silly, or even a deranged, man. Yet the teaching of St. Francis considerably elevated man in an age when he believed that he was the slave of God, powerless over his destiny. When Francis preached to the birds, he was saying that man is born with custodial responsibilities, brought to earth as God's deputy, responsible for the land and for its creatures. Francis' sermon was directed not to the birds, but rather to us. Offner's animals are born from nature and transfigured by art. As such, they speak of life, of death, and of resurrection. With his simple and gentle respect for animals, Offner gives them eloquent dignity in his art. These sculptures express reverence for life and love of beauty; they are powerful echoes of the sermon of Saint Francis.

Richard Mühlberger, *Director*
Museum of Fine Arts
Springfield, Massachusetts
September 22, 1984

ELLIOT OFFNER AT THE FORUM GALLERY

As LONG as I have known him, Elliot Offner has been fascinated by the forms of living things—among them, the shapes of fish, birds and animals, which have always been an important part of his art. In every exhibition, in one form or another, in the twenty years he has been exhibiting at the Forum Gallery, Elliot has shown carvings or castings in which he has taken loving care to animate wood or bronze through masterful technique in order to catch our eye by way of beauty of patina or liveliness of carved surface, and lead us beneath the surface to the place where the individual heart of his subject lives and beats.

Therefore, I am especially delighted to have this exhibition of Elliot Offner's "menagerie" initiated by the Museum of Fine Arts of Springfield, Massachusetts, so that others may experience the delicacy and strength which are combined in this outstanding American sculptor's work—qualities which we at the gallery have been acquainted with for so long.

I wish to thank Richard Mülhberger, Director of the Museum, and his staff for all their interest and good work.

Bella Fishko, Director
Forum Gallery

AFTERWORD

OVER *a period of as many years as I have been making sculpture, my work has had the support of many people. But two extraordinary individuals must be singled out for thanks for the incalculable benefit I have received from their encouragement. One is Rosemary, my wife, whose mind and spirit are at the center of my world, part of the wellspring of creation. All exists because of her.*

The other person is Bella Fishko, Director of Forum Gallery, whose love and knowledge of art have earned her a reputation as one of the great women of modern art. Her intelligent perception of art is matched as well by her understanding of artists, whose egos and demons can require the most demanding care. Bella is a direct and sensitive person who gives unfailing support to her artists.

The idea for this exhibition was born one day in the beautiful back room of the Forum Gallery during a conversation among Rosemary, Bella, and me. Bella observed that the animals gradually were becoming a more dominant theme for me over the last ten years, and she thought we might have a show of these works. She remembered that there was a line from Genesis *about birds and fish, to which Rosemary replied, "The fowl of the Air, the fish of the Sea, and the beasts of the Field."*

Except for two years in Europe, we had lived and worked in Western Massachusetts for 25 years. Thus, Bella and Rosemary thought that the most appropriate museum to mount and organize the exhibition would be the Springfield Museum of Fine Arts. After that, Forum Gallery would show it.

I am particularly grateful to Richard Mühlberger, Director of the Museum of Fine Arts, for responding to the initial inquiries about the show by becoming its moving force. Rosemary and I have admired Richard because of the outstanding Art enrichment of civilized life he has brought to this area through his work as Director of the Springfield Museums. We have now had a chance to work with him ourselves, an experience which has shown him to be as kind, generous, tireless and reassuring as he is knowledgeable of art and people. Richard's staff must be thanked also, for their remarkable patience and warm-spirited willingness to do whatever was asked of them.

In 1960 I joined the faculty at Smith, the College from which my wife had graduated some years earlier. There I had the excellent fortune to find an Art Department composed of many artists and art historians whose deep knowledge accompanied a passion for the art object. From them I learned much and I continue to learn more. Furthermore, Smith College has always supported my work, with time off and monetary assistance, including a grant to assist in the mounting of this exhibition.

Rocky Stinehour and Meriden-Stinehour Inc. also must be thanked for accepting my art as partial payment for the production of this catalogue.

Finally, I have a word to say about my work. A love of books is probably my oldest link to art. Books, and in time, letter form and printing have remained a powerful interest, even though I spend far more time making sculpture. I am fortunate in finding expression through teaching these graphic forms, although I always find some time to draw and carve letters or to design a broadside.

If for many years, as others have said, my sculpture was more about the human condition, I see my work increasingly as being interpretations of creatures from the world in which we live. To make art from nature, I believe an artist must have a special penetrating vision of his subject to see what others have not seen. This he must translate to his medium, so that all who encounter his work will have a new reality revealed, a universe expanded. Such penetrating vision comes not only through careful scrutiny of nature but also through the constant investigation of the ways in which greater talents achieved their vision.

Thus, Henry Moore's endless hours before the Parthenon marbles in the British Museum affected his new interpretations of the reclining woman; likewise, Alberto Giacometti's magnificent figures are a poignant reminder of Greek and Etruscan antecedents, while Giacomo Manzu's brilliant bas-reliefs recall Donatello's late low reliefs and his bold willingness to cross between raised form and drawing.

What I do then is study with intensity the creatures I want to interpret. I photograph them, I draw them and I try to see their inner life and form. It is nature primarily that fires my sculpture, although I always study significant interpretations of other times as well as the present. This visual enquiry is part of the fabric of creation, a process which informs and humbles.

Elliot Offner
Northampton, Massachusetts, 1984

Measurements are given in inches, height preceding width and depth for sculpture, height preceding width for works on paper. Image measurements are given for works on paper. All bronze sculptures are reserved for an edition of six. Where more than one has been cast, the edition number is listed.

All sculptures, drawings, and woodcuts are from the collection of Forum Gallery, except where noted.

SCULPTURE:

1.
DAPEDIUM GRANULATUM, 1971
Bronze (relief), Edition: 2/6, 15 x 21

2.
RHINOBATUS BUGASIACUS, 1971
Bronze (relief), Edition: 1/6, 17 x 23
Lent by Dr. and Mrs. Michael Hume

3.
LEPIDOTUS ELVENSIS, 1971
Bronze (relief), Edition: 2/6, 10 x 14

4.
FISH, 1972
Wood (Butternut), 32 x 8½ x 28½
Private Collector

5.
SKULL #2, 1973
Bronze, Edition: 2/6, 12¾ x 7½ x 10

6.
SKULL #1, 1973
Bronze, Edition: 2/6, 7 x 7 x 16

7.
HEADS & SKULL IN METAMORPHOSIS, 1974
Bronze, Edition: 2/6, 7½ x 4 x 5½

8.
GREAT WOOD SKULL, 1974
Wood (Maple), 45½ x 18½ x 17

9.
MASTURUS VERUCOSUS, 1974
Bronze (relief), Edition: 3/6, 14 x 15

10.
HATCHET FISH, 1975
Wood (Birch), 26 x 11 x 45
Lent by Mr. and Mrs. Marvin Flowerman

11.
Maquette for *ST. FRANCIS AS A YOUTH*, 1976   Bronze, Edition: 2/6, 17 x 7½ x 11

12.
THE ARTIST'S SON AS ST. FRANCIS, 1976
Bronze, 12 x 7 x 16
Lent by Rosemary O'Connell Offner

13.
MYTHICAL BIRD, 1976
Wood (Birch), 22 x 39¼ x 16

14.
HATCHET FISH, 1975/77
Bronze, 23 x 9 x 42

15.
LION, 1977
Bronze, Edition: 2/6, 10 x 5½ x 15

16.
COCKEREL #1, 1978
Bronze, Edition: 2/6, 16 x 10 x 22

17.
BITTERN, 1978
Bronze, Edition: 3/6, 17¼ x 5 x 8½
Lent by Mr. and Mrs. Manuel Baker

18.
GRIFFIN, 1978
Bronze, 12 x 5 x 14

19.
DOVE OF ST. FRANCIS, 1978
Bronze, Edition: 3/6, 6½ x 5¾ x 11

20.
RUFF, 1978
Bronze, Edition: 2/6, 11 x 7¼ x 14

21.
LION OF JUDAH, 1979
Wood (Cherry), 20 x 11 x 39.

22. (frontispiece)
COCKEREL #2, 1982
Bronze, 31 x 10 x 23

23. (fig. 23 & back cover)
KITE, 1983
Bronze, 30 x 23 x 37

24.
AMERICAN BITTERN, 1983
Wood (Poplar, Cherry, Maple), 42 x 14 x 24

25.
ASIAN PHEASANT, 1983
Bronze, 17 x 10 x 28

26.
PHEASANT, 1978/84
Bronze, 19 x 7 x 38
Lent by Deerfield Academy

27.
COCKEREL, 1984
Plaster (relief), $27^7/8$ x $20^7/8$

28.
Maquette for *ANGEL FISH*, 1984
Bronze, Edition: 1/6, $18^1/4$ x $3^3/4$ x $17^3/8$
Lent by Dr. and Mrs. Kristaps J. Keggi

29. (fig. 29 & front cover)
ANGEL FISH, 1984
Wood (Cherry), $41^1/2$ x 41 x 16

30.
TURKEY, 1984
Bronze, 32 x $25^1/2$ x $20^1/2$

WORKING DRAWINGS for SCULPTURE:

31.
GREAT WOOD SKULL, 1974
Pencil, $46^1/4$ x $24^1/2$

32.
GREAT WOOD SKULL, 1974
Pencil, $51^1/8$ x $20^7/8$

33.
HATCHET FISH, 1975
Pencil, $19^7/8$ x 40

34.
THE ARTIST'S SON AS ST. FRANCIS, 1976
Pencil, $30^1/2$ x $21^1/2$
Lent by Rosemary O'Connell Offner

35.
AWAKENING, 1982
Pencil, $27^1/4$ x $29^1/2$
Lent by Museum of Fine Arts, Springfield, Massachusetts

36.
TURKEY, 1984
Pencil, 23 x 35

37.
TURKEY, 1984
Pencil, 23 x 35

WOODCUTS:

38.
GRIFFIN, 1974
2 Color Blocks, Edition: 2/100, $7^1/2$ x $9^1/2$

39.
LION OF JUDAH, 1975
3 Color Blocks, Artist's Proof, 5 x $9^1/4$

40.
PORCUPINE, 1975
3 Color Blocks, Edition: 1/75, $11^1/4$ x $14^1/2$

41.
WILD BOAR, 1975
2 Color Blocks, Artist's Proof, 8 x 10

42.
GIRAFFE, 1976
1 Color Block, Artist's Proof, $23^1/4$ x 15

43.
OLIVE TREE, 1976
1 Color Block, Artist's Proof, 6 x $3^1/4$

44.
WILD ROSEMARY, 1977
1 Color Block, Artist's Proof, $6^3/4$ x $3^1/2$

45.
MONARCH BUTTERFLY, 1982
Hand Colored, Artist's Proof, 18 x $14^3/8$

46.
TREES ON HAMPSTEAD HEATH, 1982
3 Color Blocks, Artist's Proof, $12^1/2$ x $19^3/4$

47.
TURKEY, 1982
2 Color Blocks, Artist's Proof, 20 x $18^1/4$

48.
WHOOPING CRANE, 1976/82
2 Color Blocks, Artist's Proof, 19 x $12^1/2$

49.
ACACIA TREE, 1984
6 Color Blocks, Artist's Proof, $25^7/8$ x $17^1/4$

50.
TWO TREES ON HAMPSTEAD HEATH, 1984
3 Color Blocks, Artist's Proof, 23 x 17

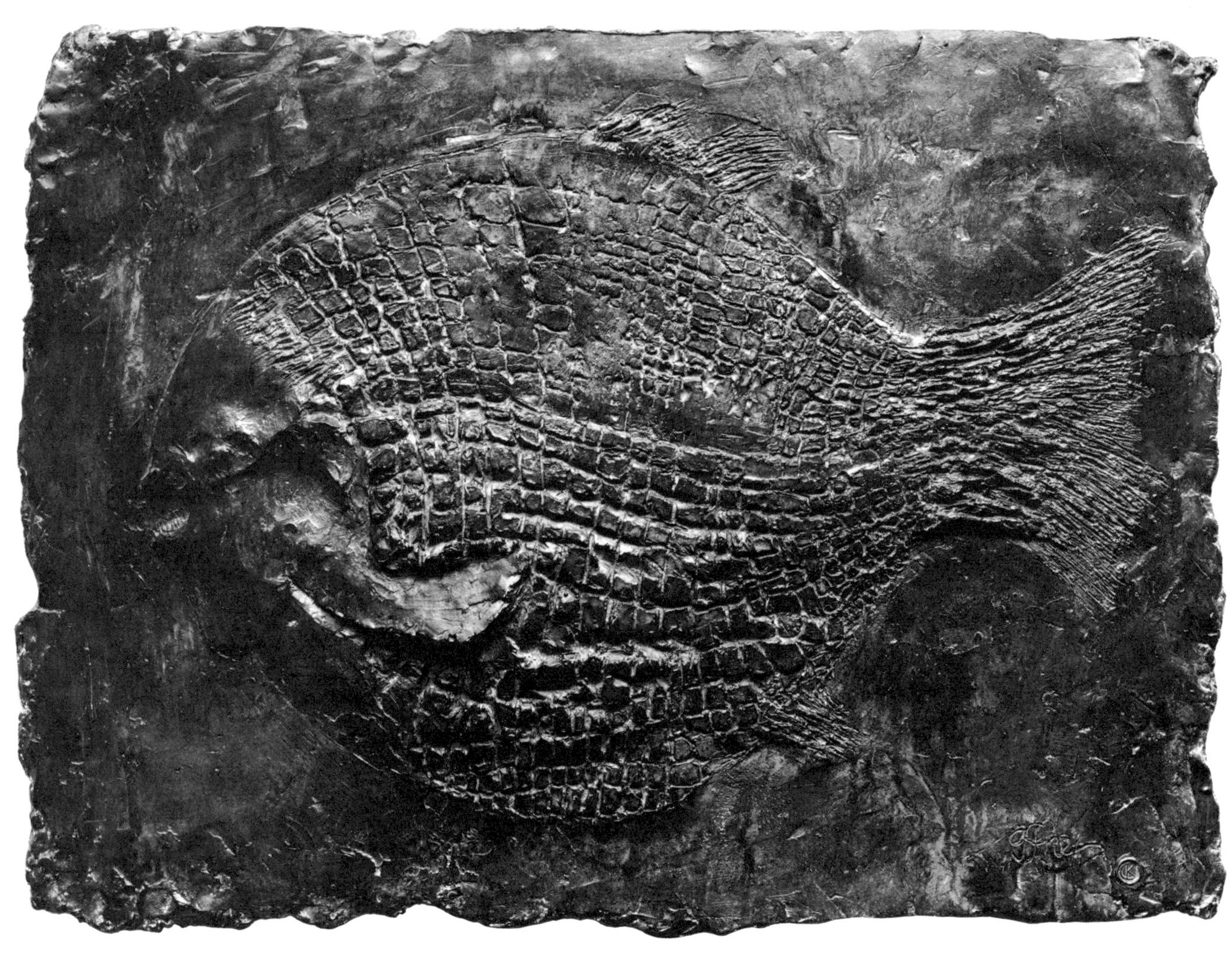

1. *DAPEDIUM GRANULATUM*, 1971, Bronze (relief), 15 x 21

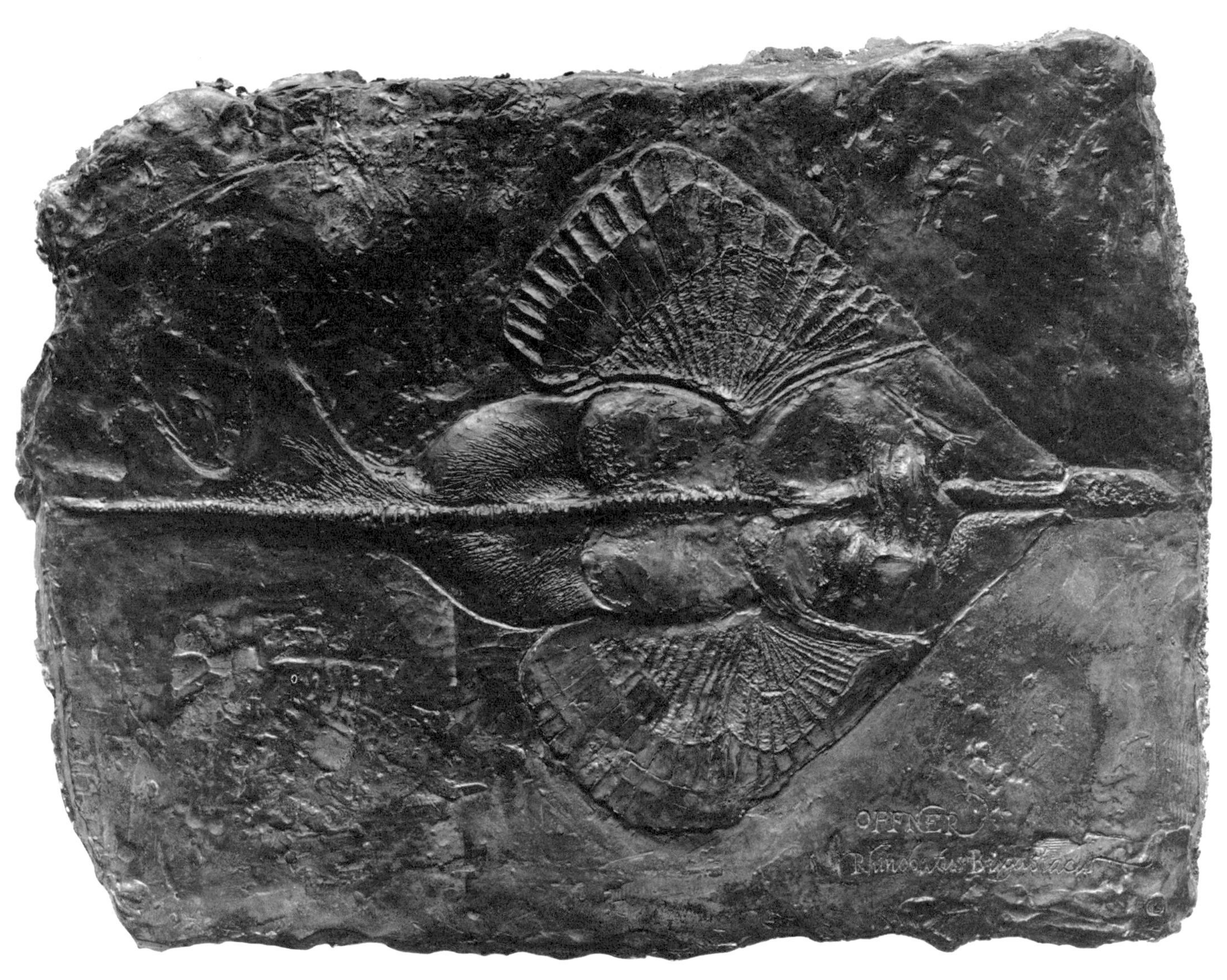

2. *RHINOBATUS BUGASIACUS*, 1971, Bronze (relief), 17 x 23

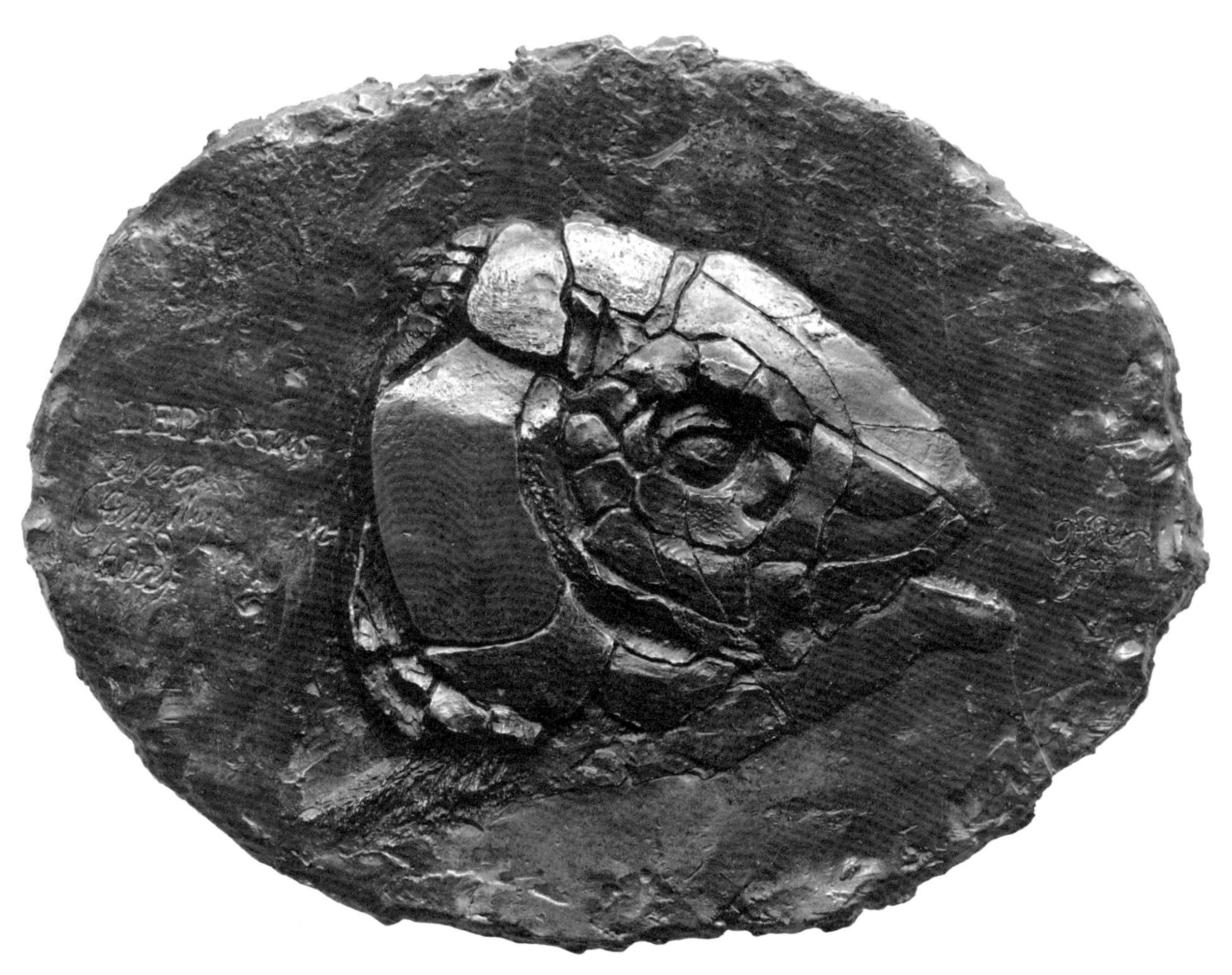

3. *LEPIDOTUS ELVENSIS*, 1971, Bronze (relief), 10 x 14

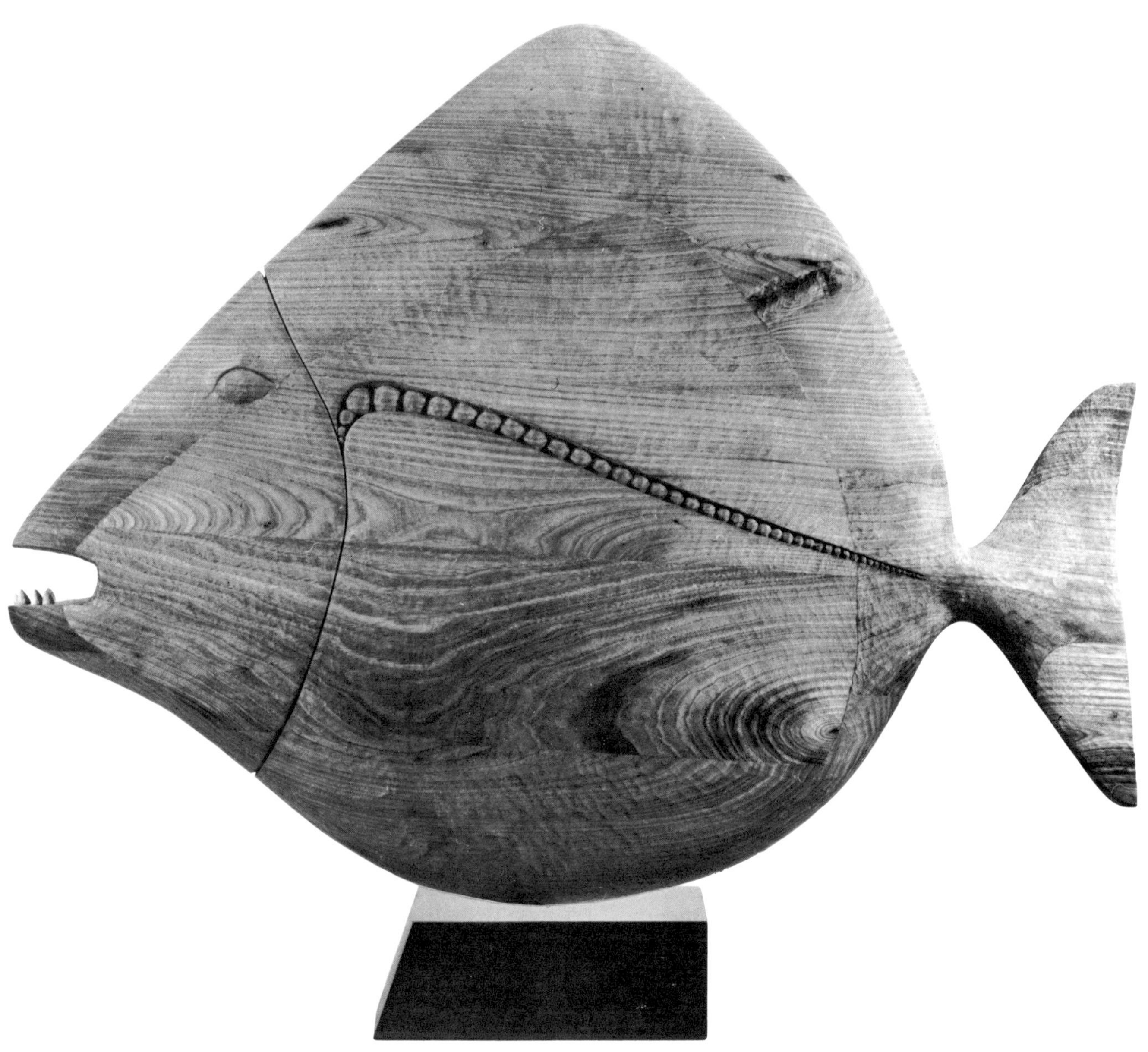

4. *FISH*, 1972, Wood (Butternut), 32 x 8¹/₂ x 28¹/₂

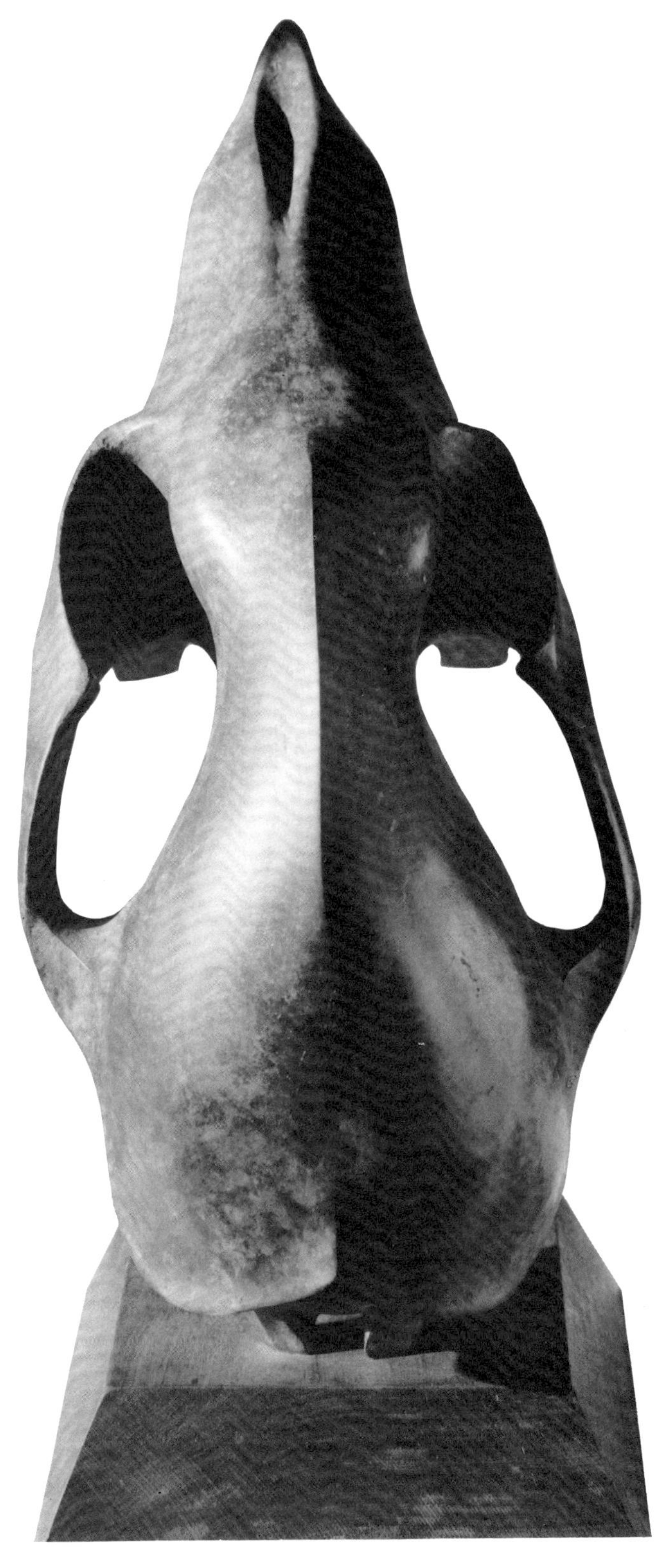

5. *SKULL #2*, 1973, Bronze, 12³/4 x 7¹/2 x 10

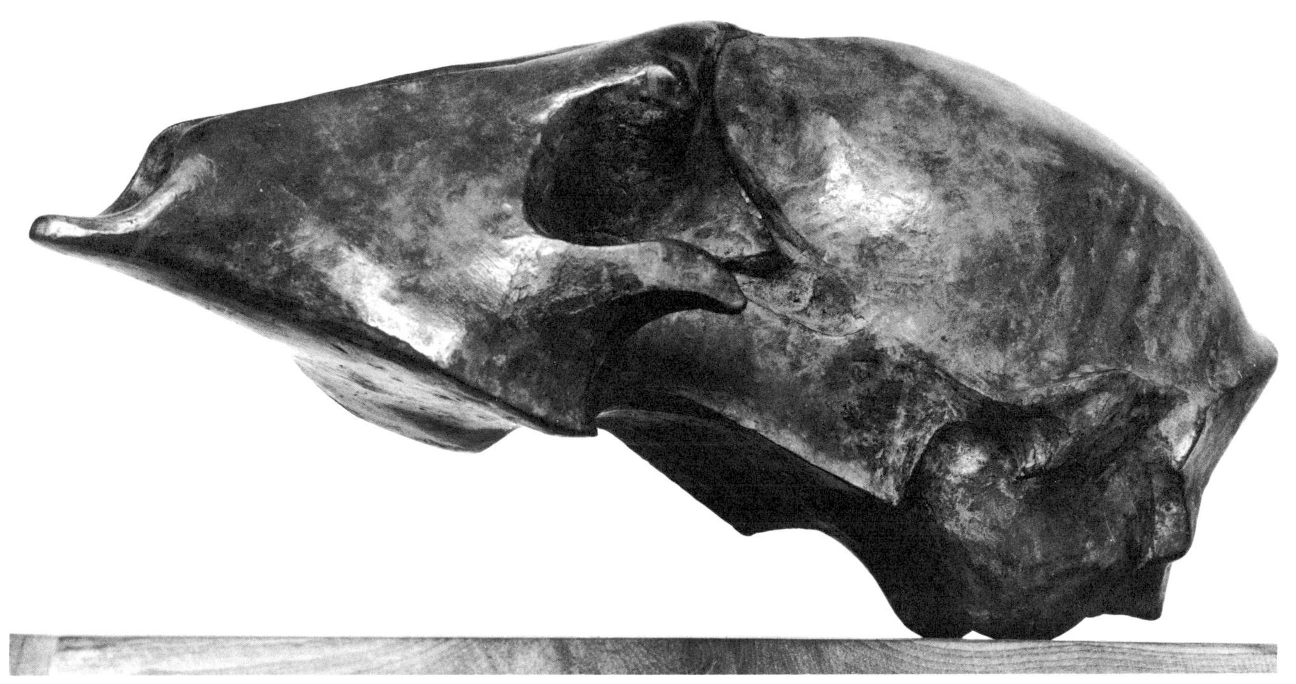

6. *SKULL #1*, 1973, Bronze, 7 x 7 x 16

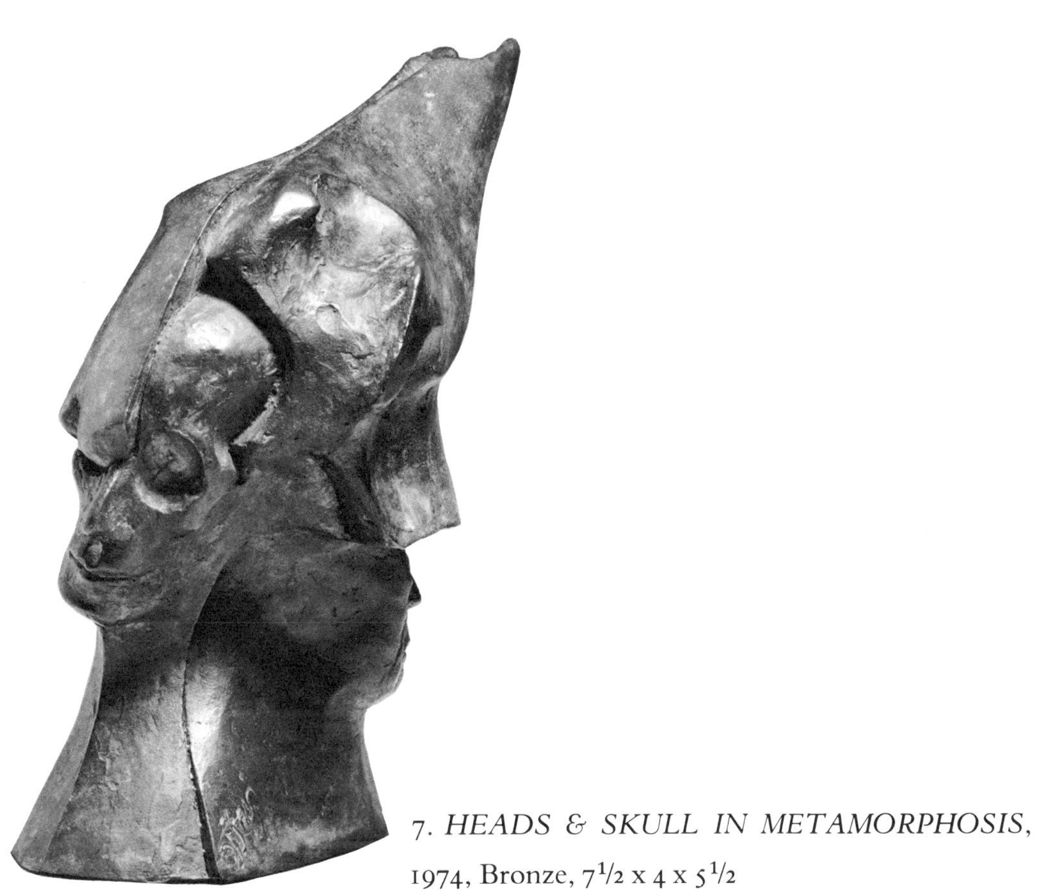

7. *HEADS & SKULL IN METAMORPHOSIS*, 1974, Bronze, 7$^{1}/_{2}$ x 4 x 5$^{1}/_{2}$

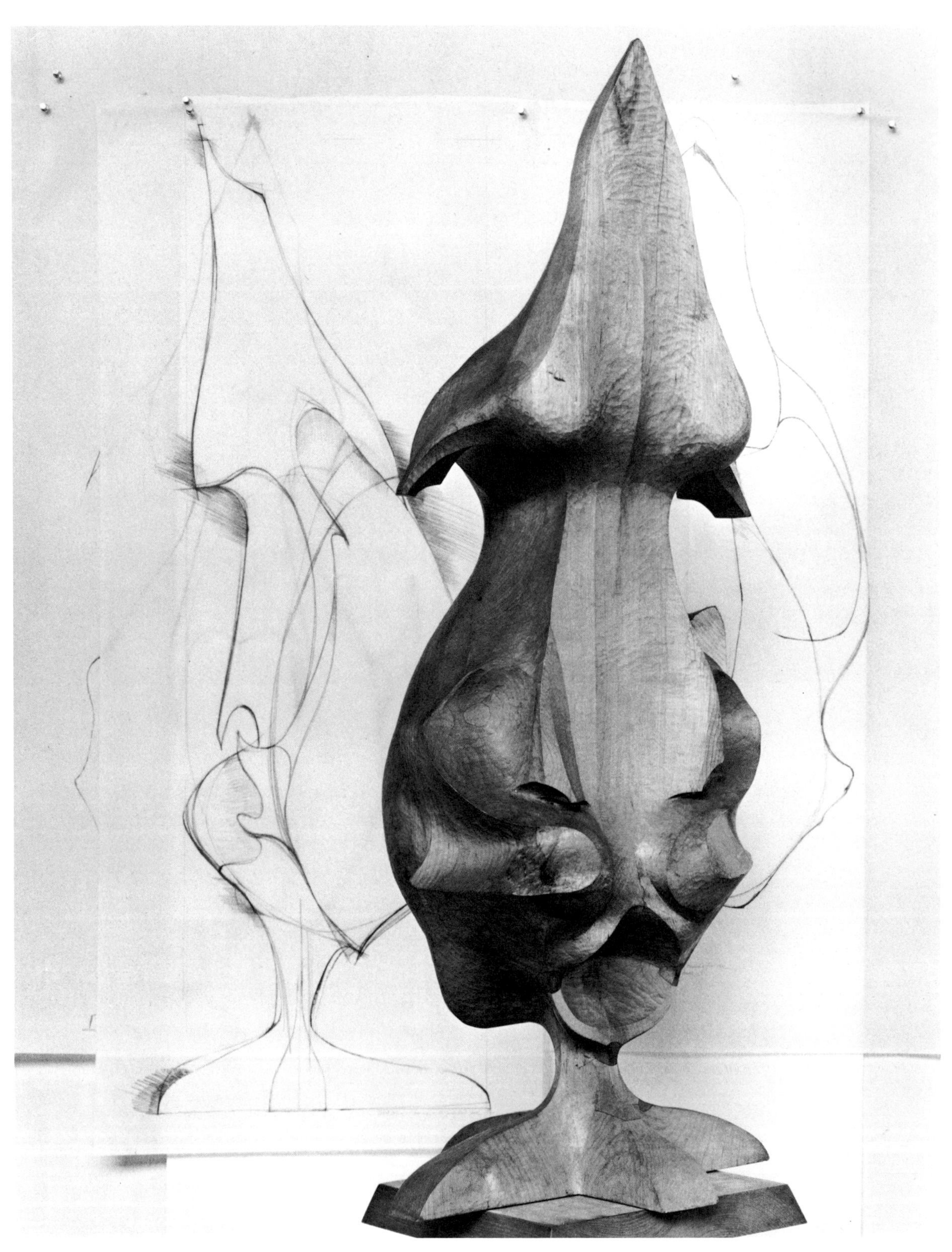

8. *GREAT WOOD SKULL*, 1974, Wood (Maple), 45¹/₂ x 18¹/₂ x 17

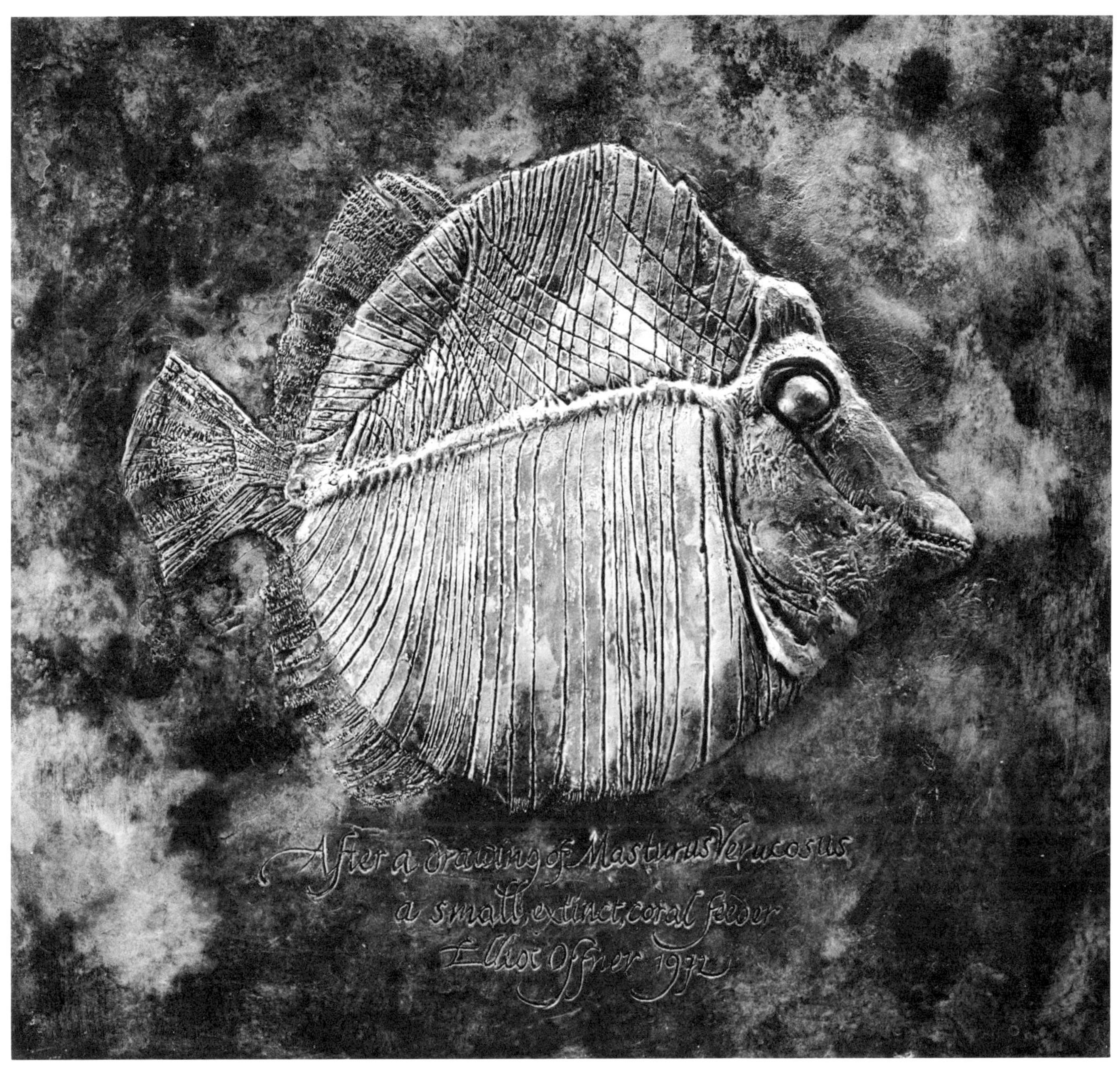

9. *MASTURUS VERUCOSUS*, 1974, Bronze (relief), 14 x 15

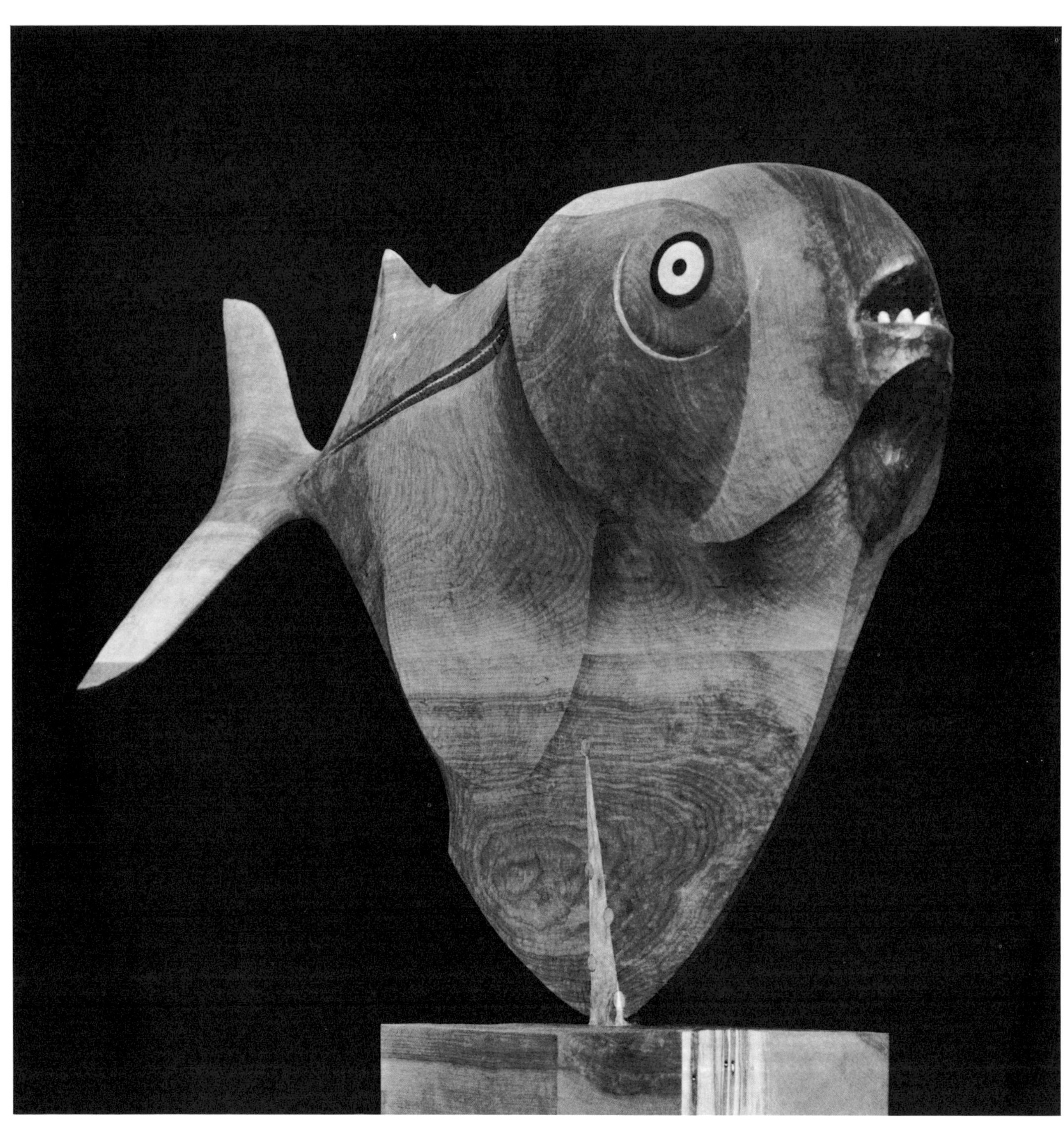

10. *HATCHET FISH*, 1975, Wood (Birch), 26 x 11 x 45

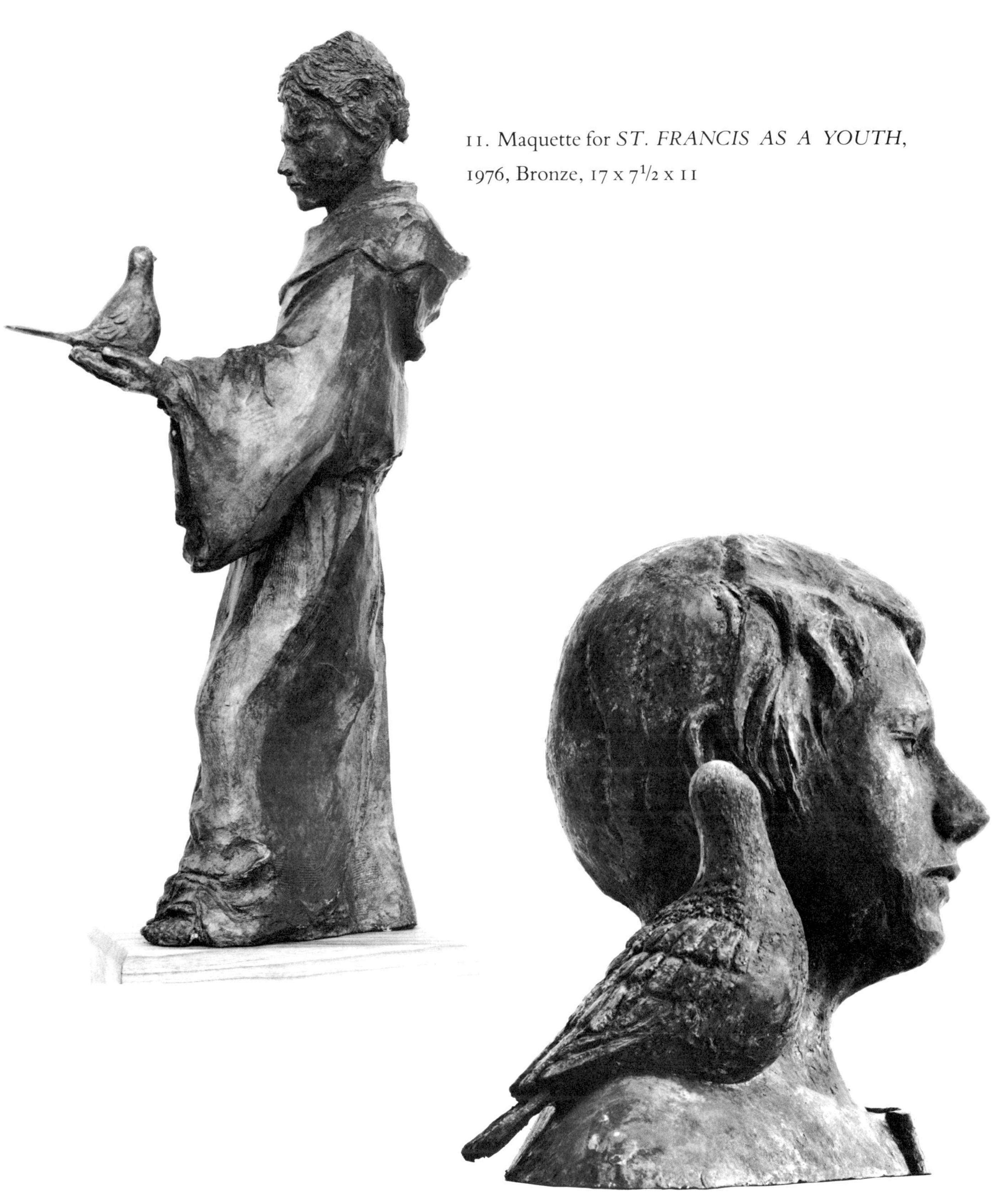

11. Maquette for *ST. FRANCIS AS A YOUTH*, 1976, Bronze, 17 x 7½ x 11

12. *THE ARTIST'S SON AS ST. FRANCIS*, 1976, Bronze, 12 x 7 x 16

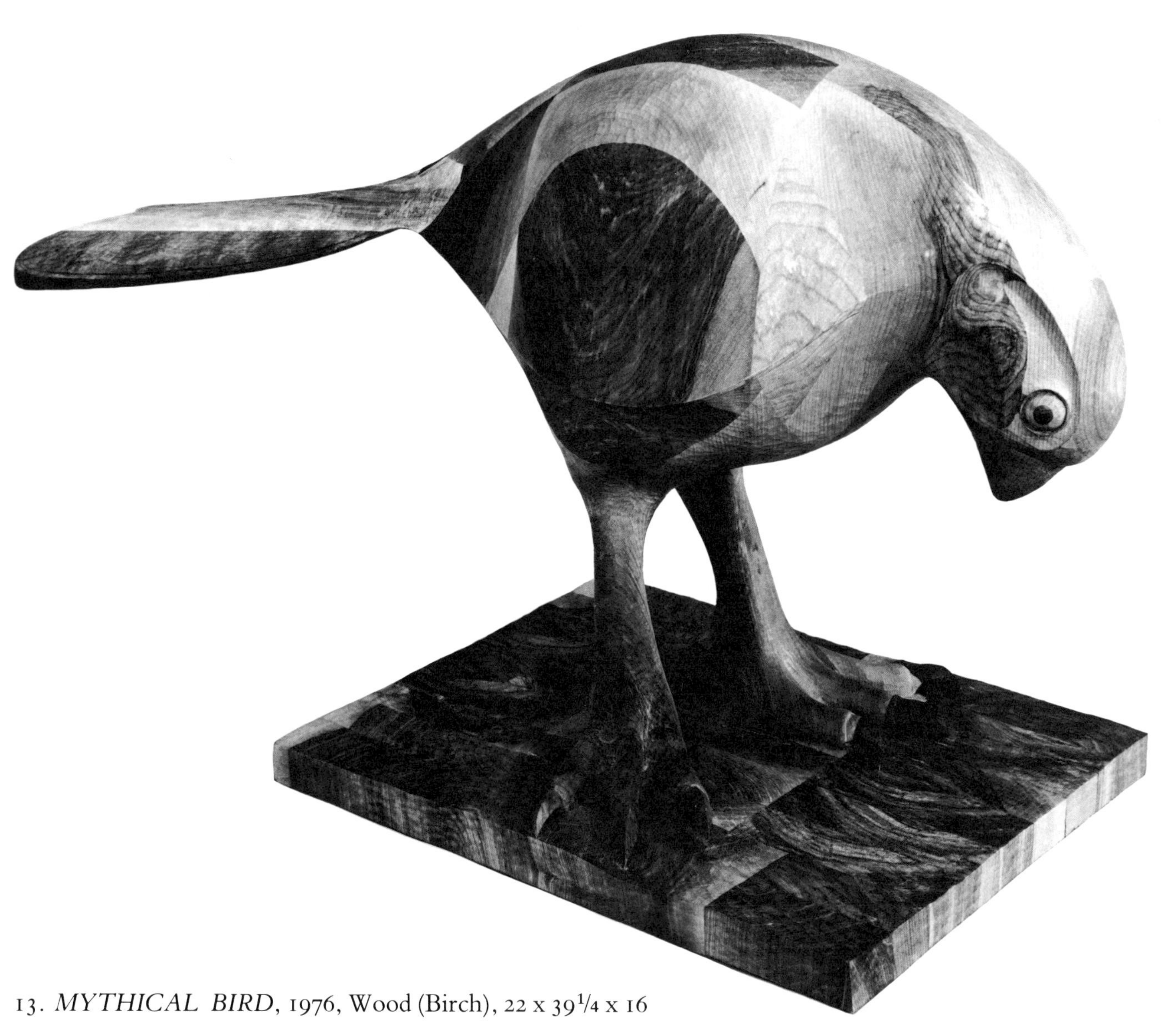

13. *MYTHICAL BIRD*, 1976, Wood (Birch), 22 x 39¼ x 16

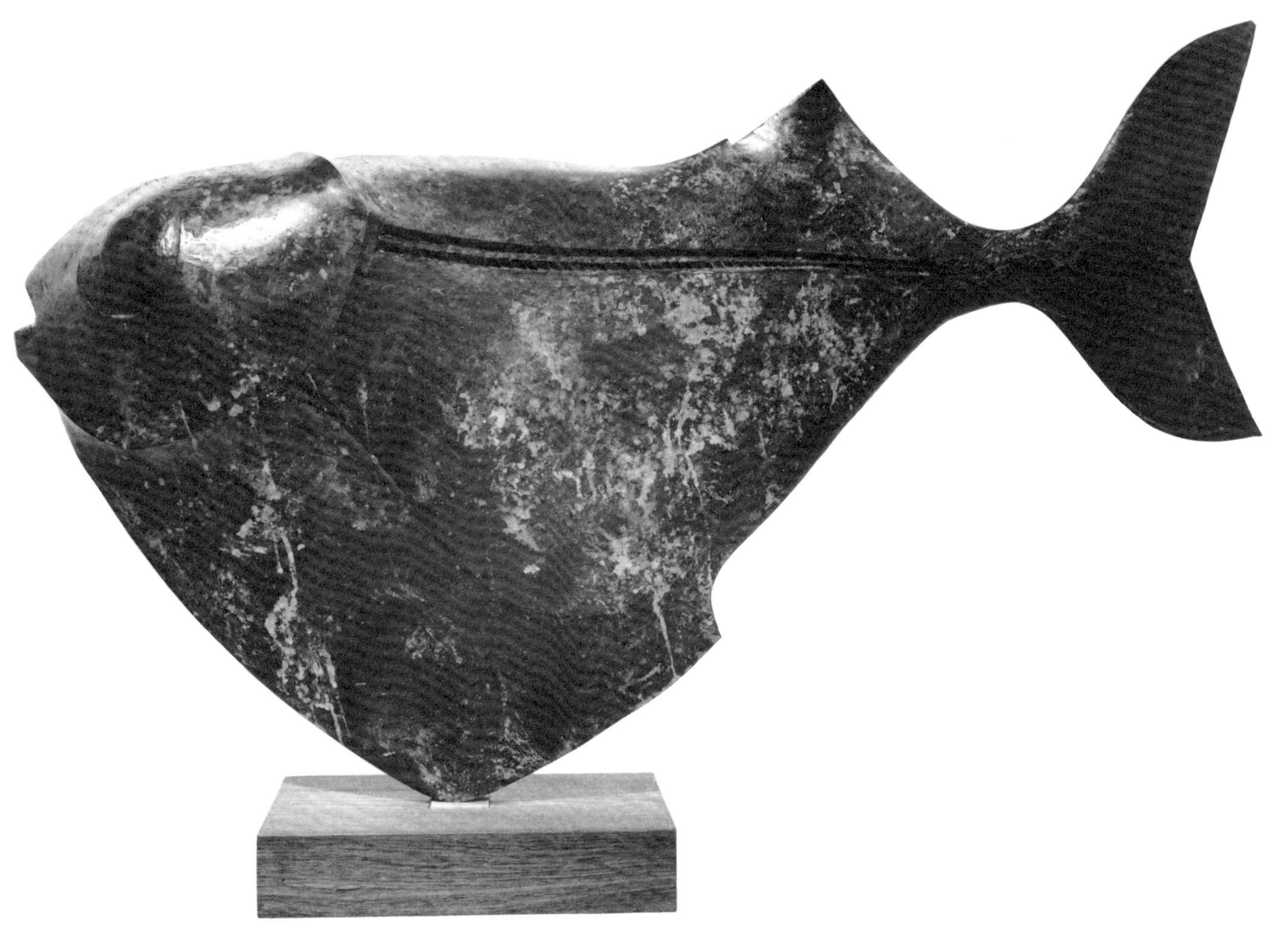

14. *HATCHET FISH*, 1975/77, Bronze, 23 x 9 x 42

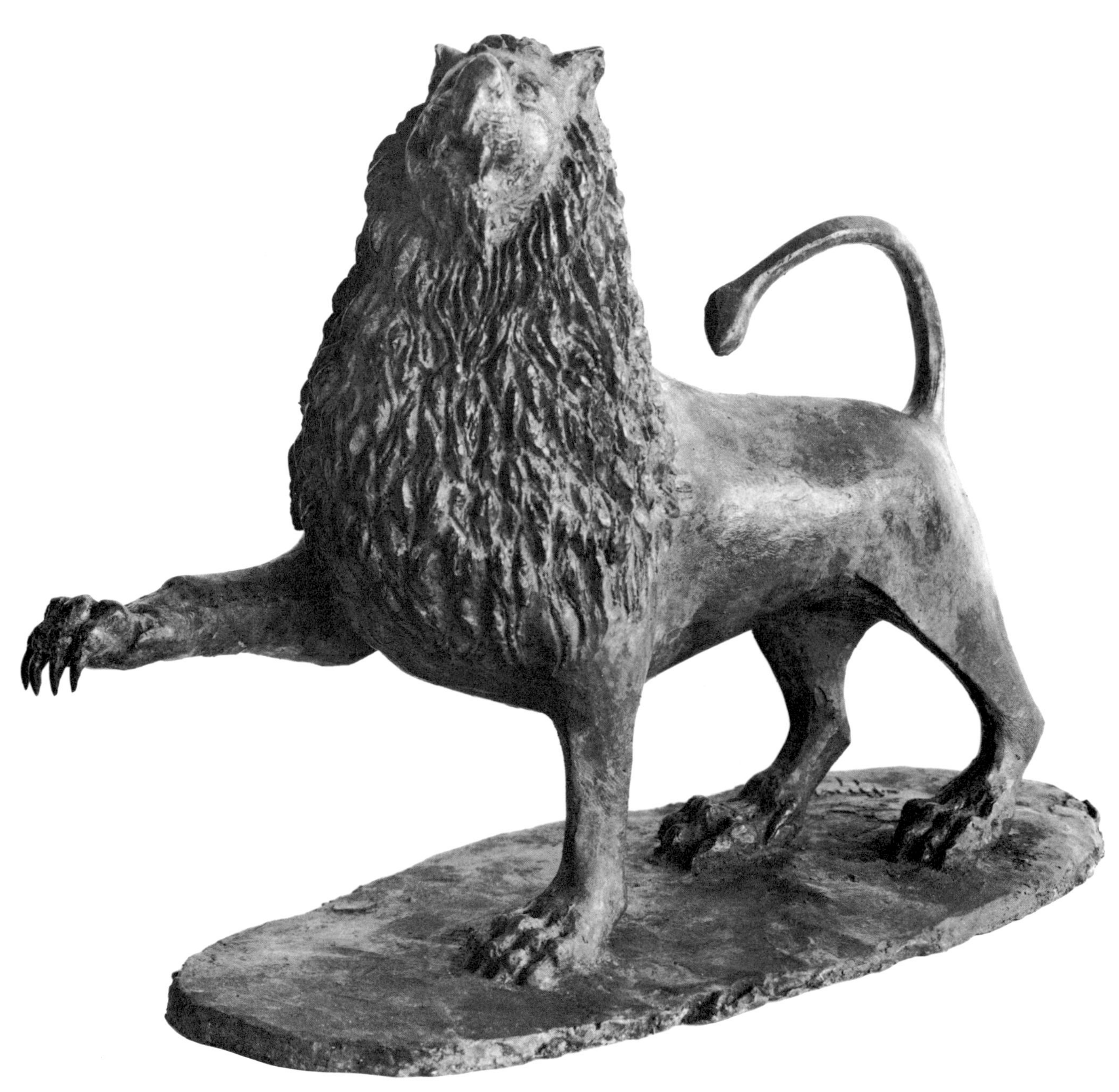

15. *LION*, 1977, Bronze, 10 x 5$\frac{1}{2}$ x 15

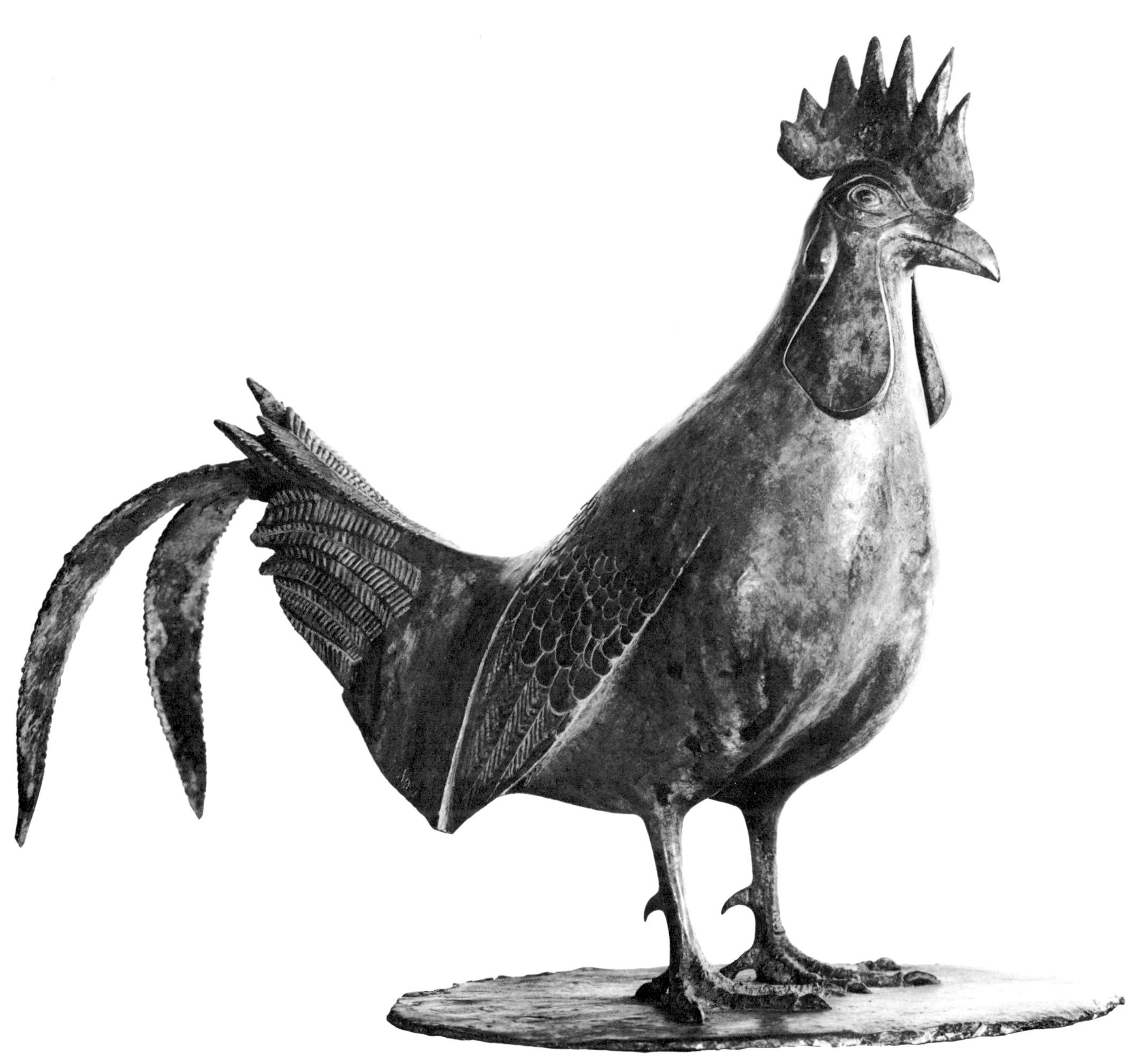

16. *COCKEREL #1*, 1978, Bronze, 16 x 10 x 22

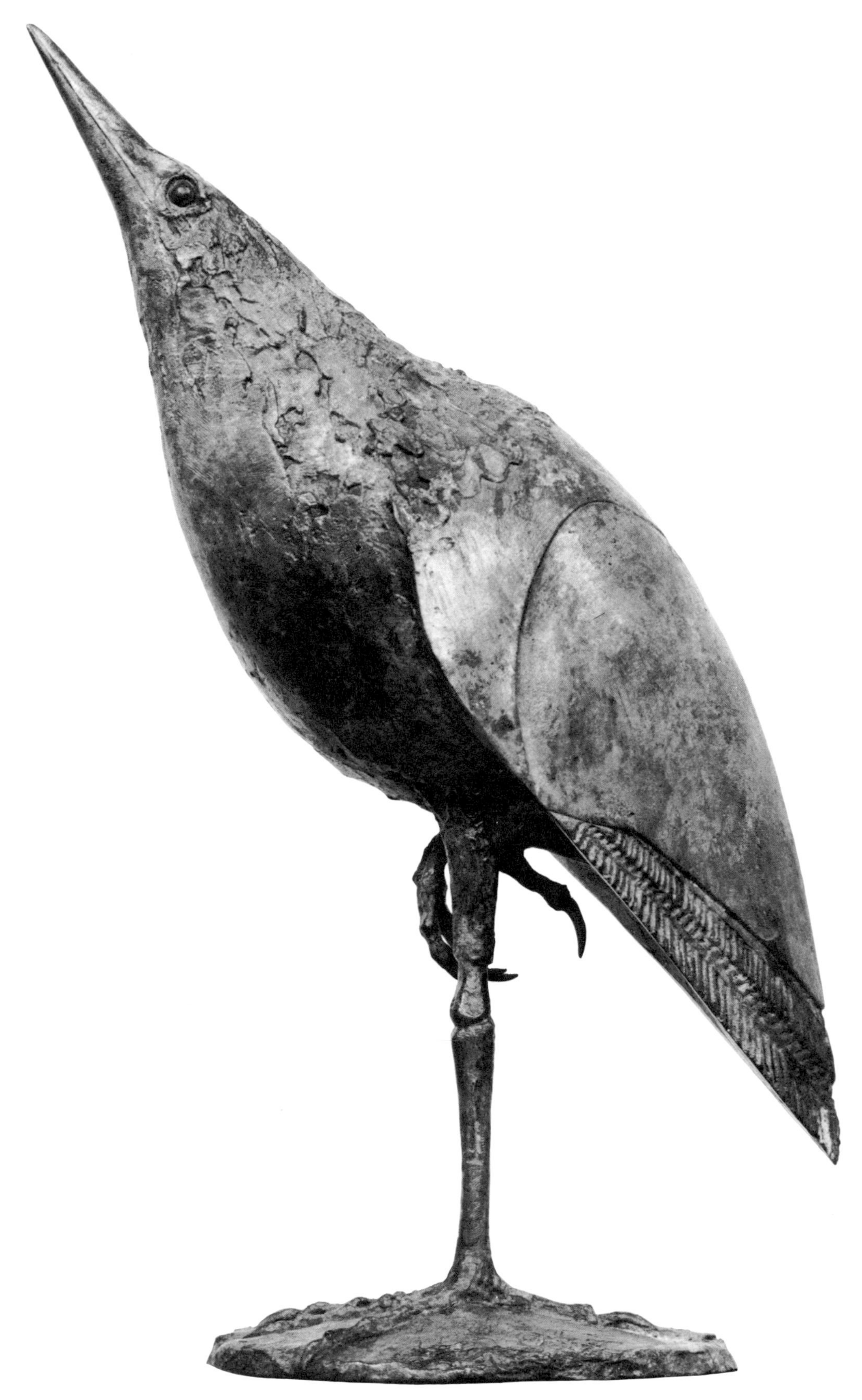

17. *BITTERN*, 1978, Bronze, 17$^{1}/_{4}$ x 5 x 8$^{1}/_{2}$

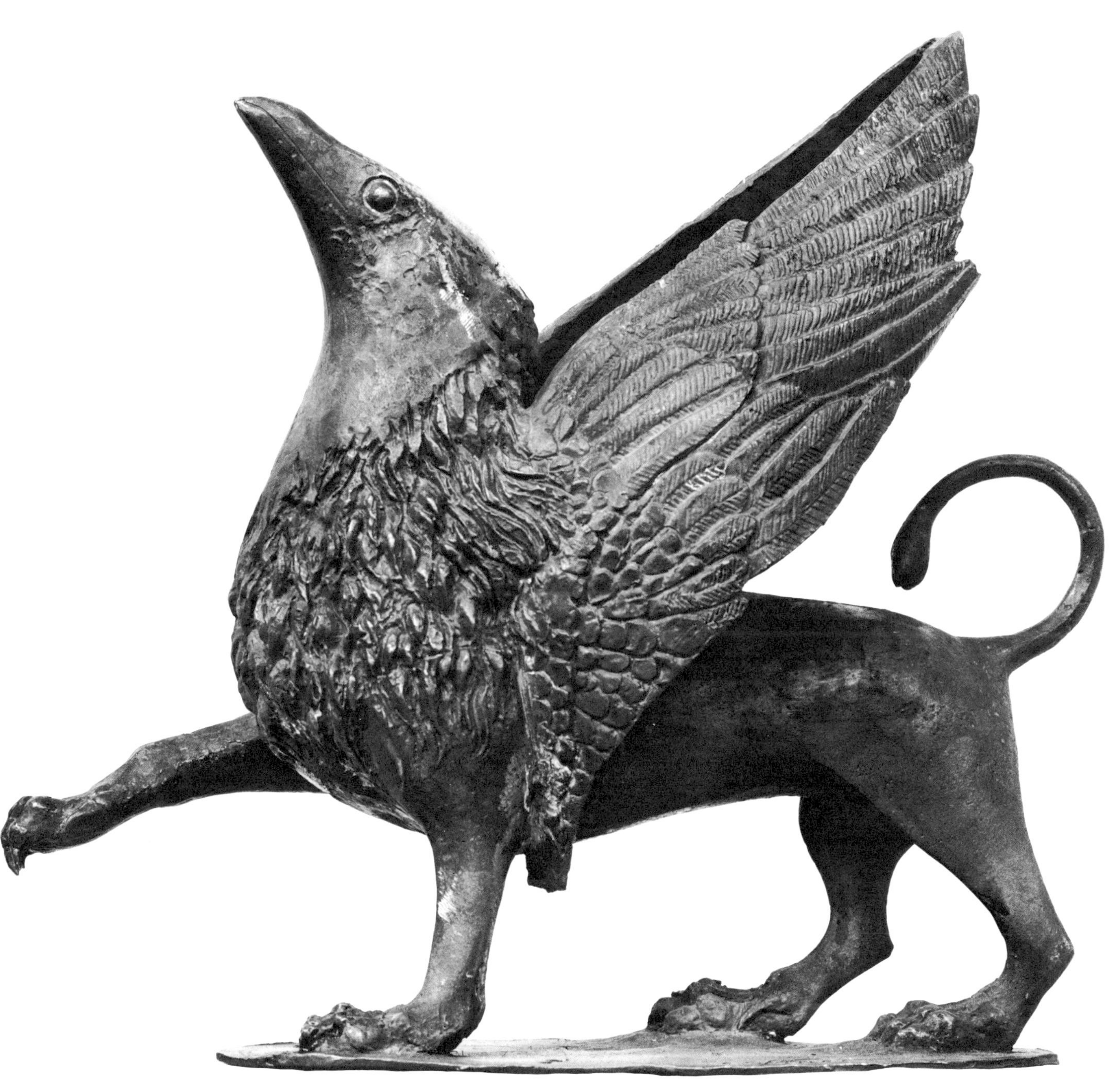

18. *GRIFFIN*, 1978, Bronze, 12 x 5 x 14

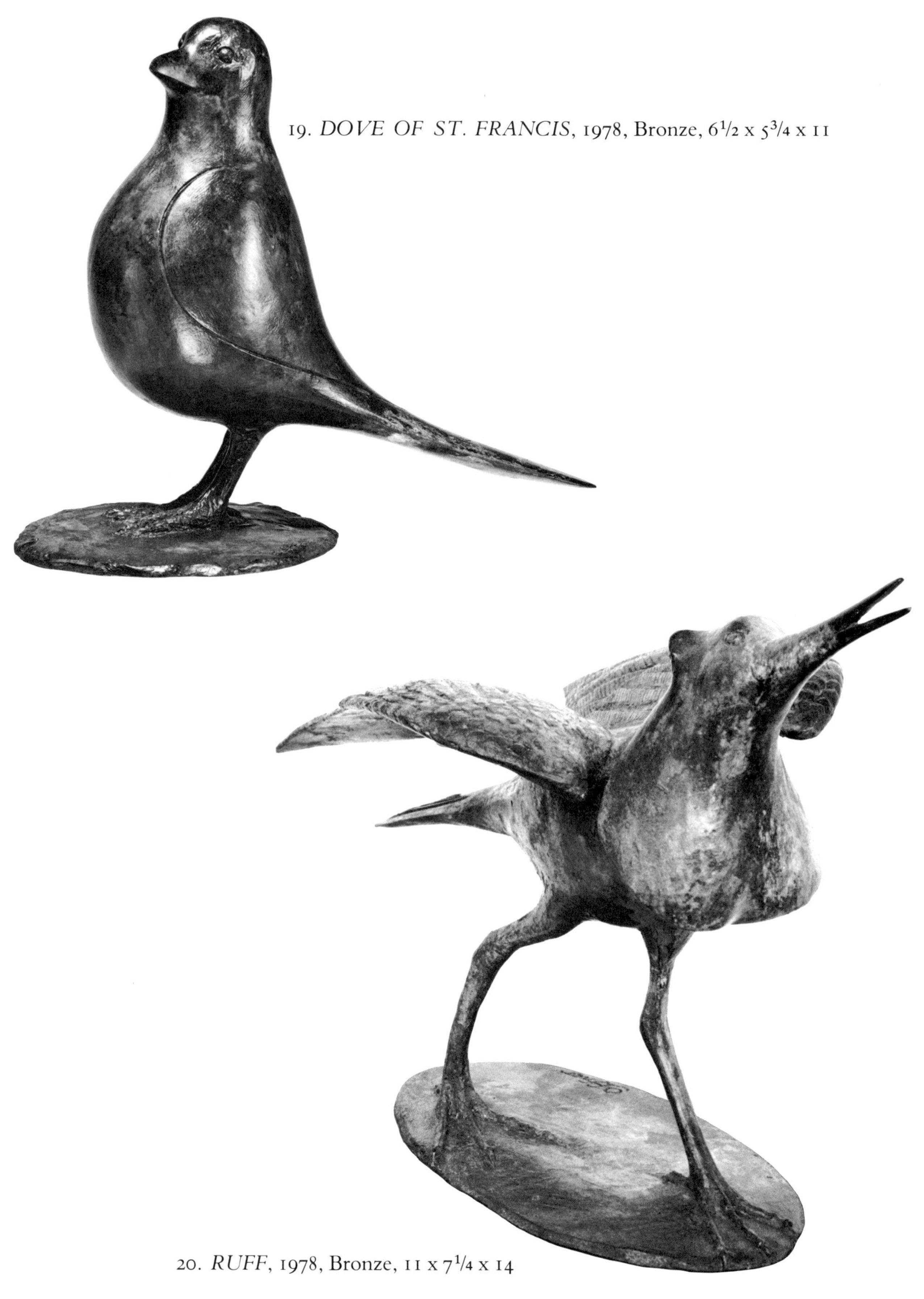

19. *DOVE OF ST. FRANCIS*, 1978, Bronze, 6$\frac{1}{2}$ x 5$\frac{3}{4}$ x 11

20. *RUFF*, 1978, Bronze, 11 x 7$\frac{1}{4}$ x 14

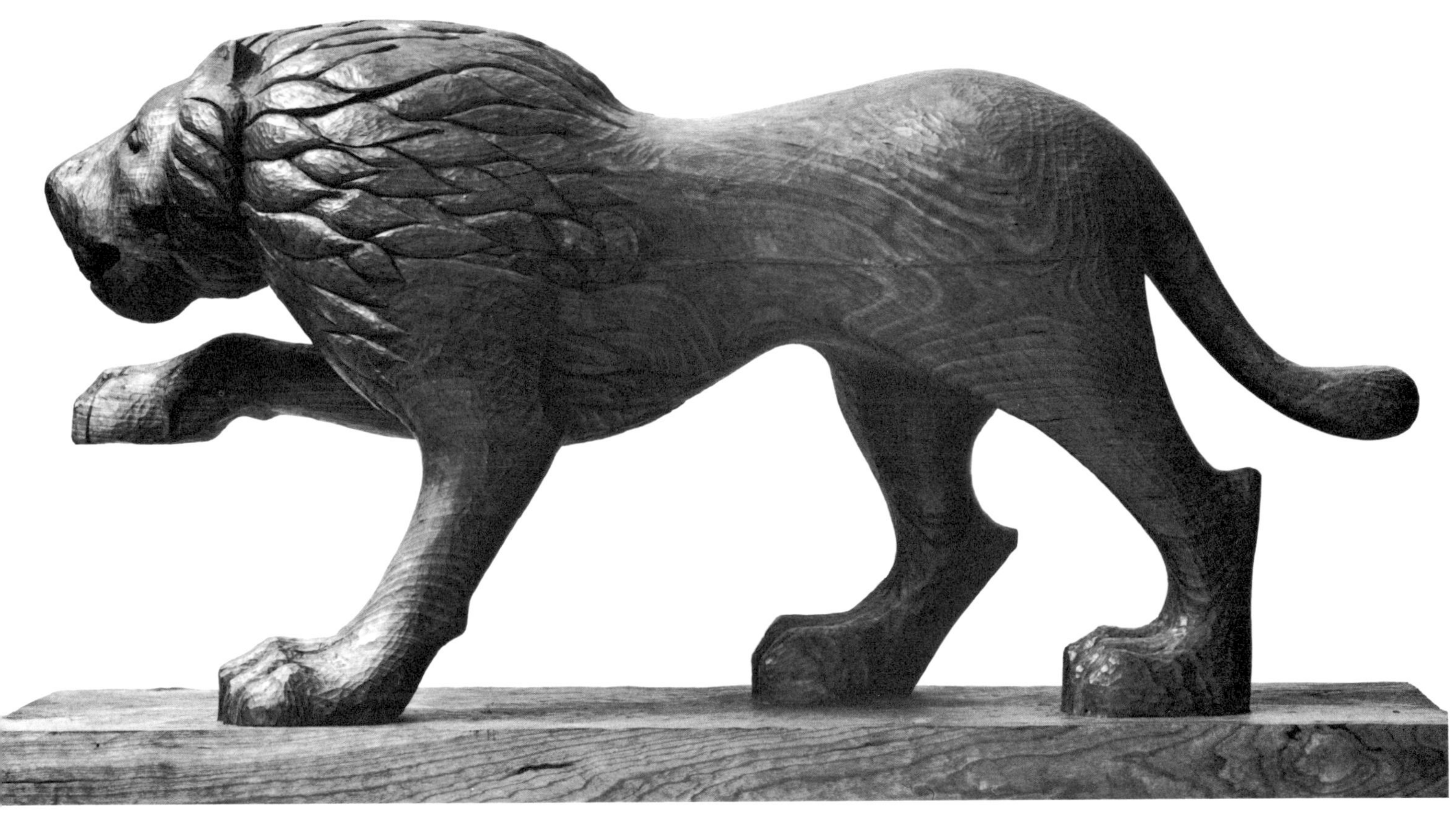

21. *LION OF JUDAH*, 1979, Wood (Cherry), 20 x 11 x 39

22. *COCKEREL #2*, 1982, Bronze, 31 x 10 x 23 (*frontispiece illustration*)

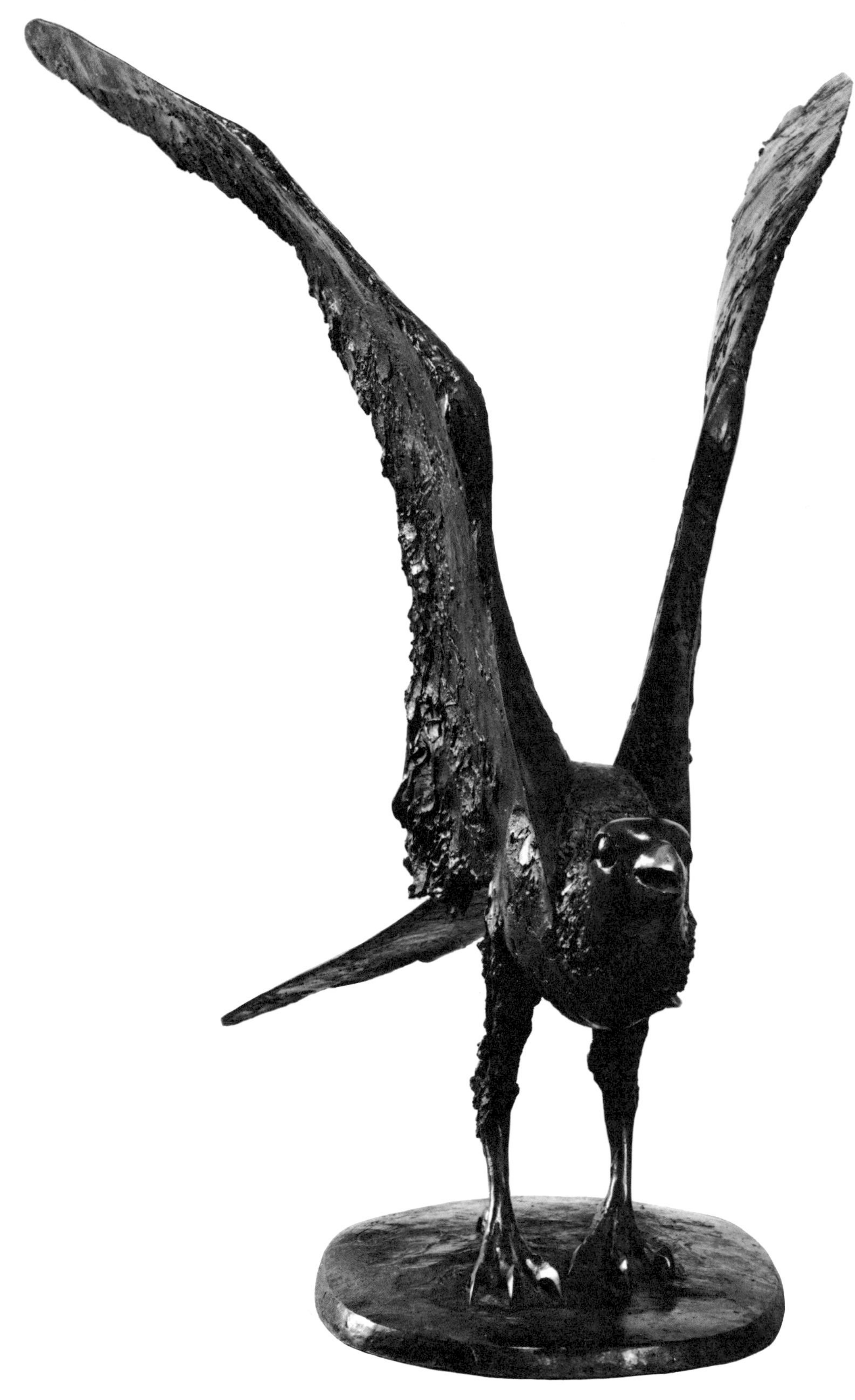

23. *KITE*, 1983, Bronze, 30 x 23 x 37

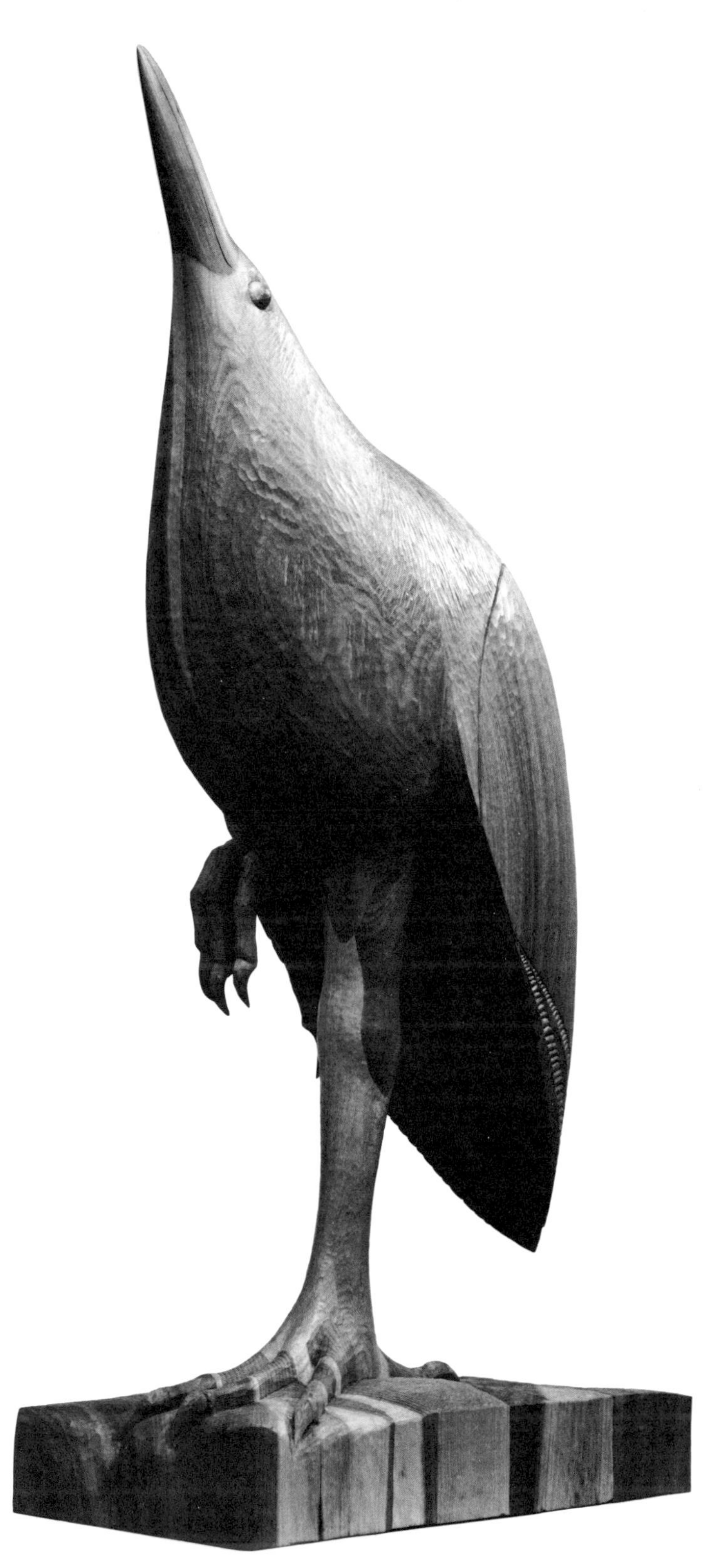

24. *AMERICAN BITTERN*, 1983, Wood (Poplar, Cherry, Maple), 42 x 14 x 24

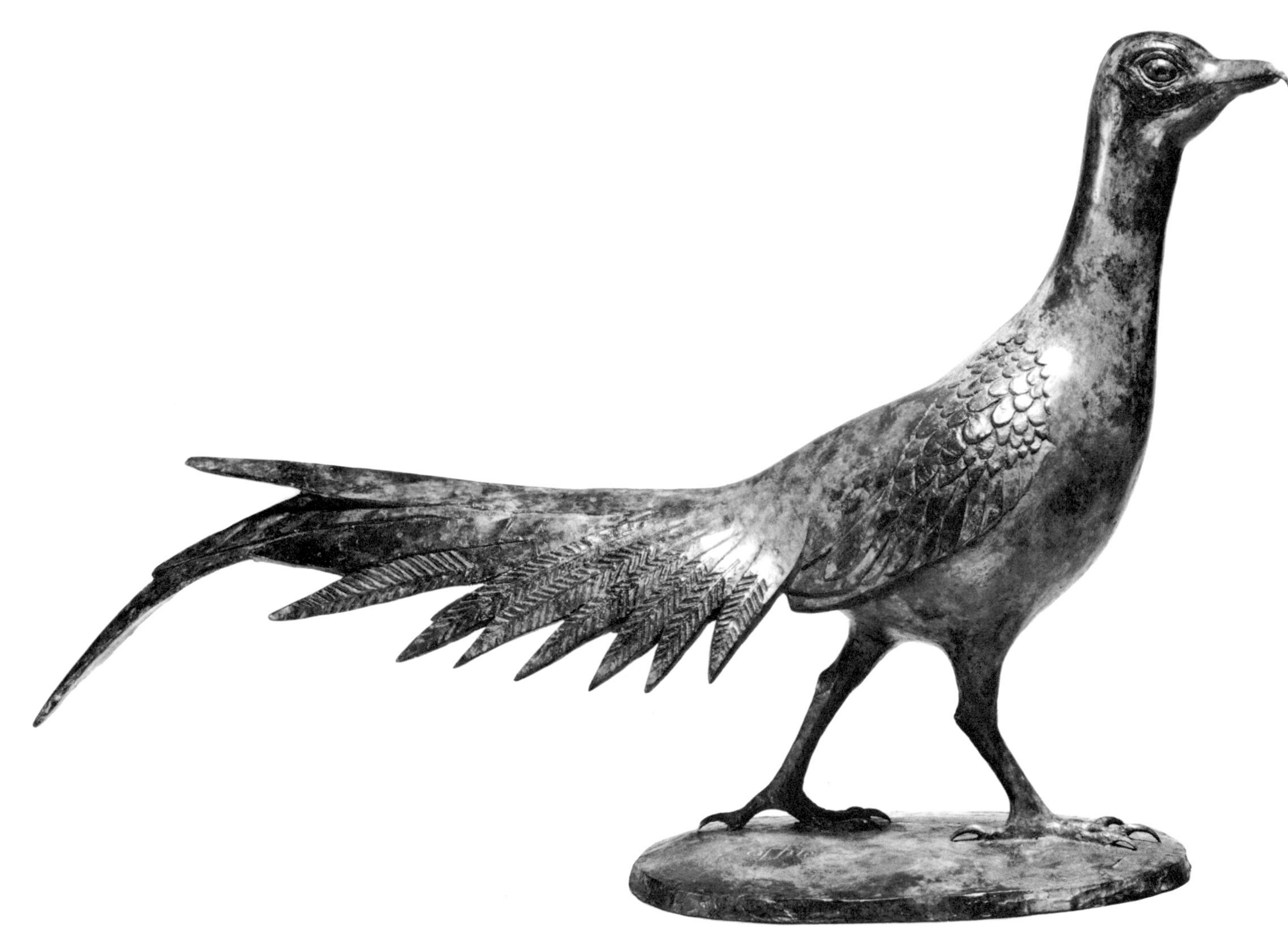

25. *ASIAN PHEASANT*, 1983, Bronze, 17 x 10 x 28

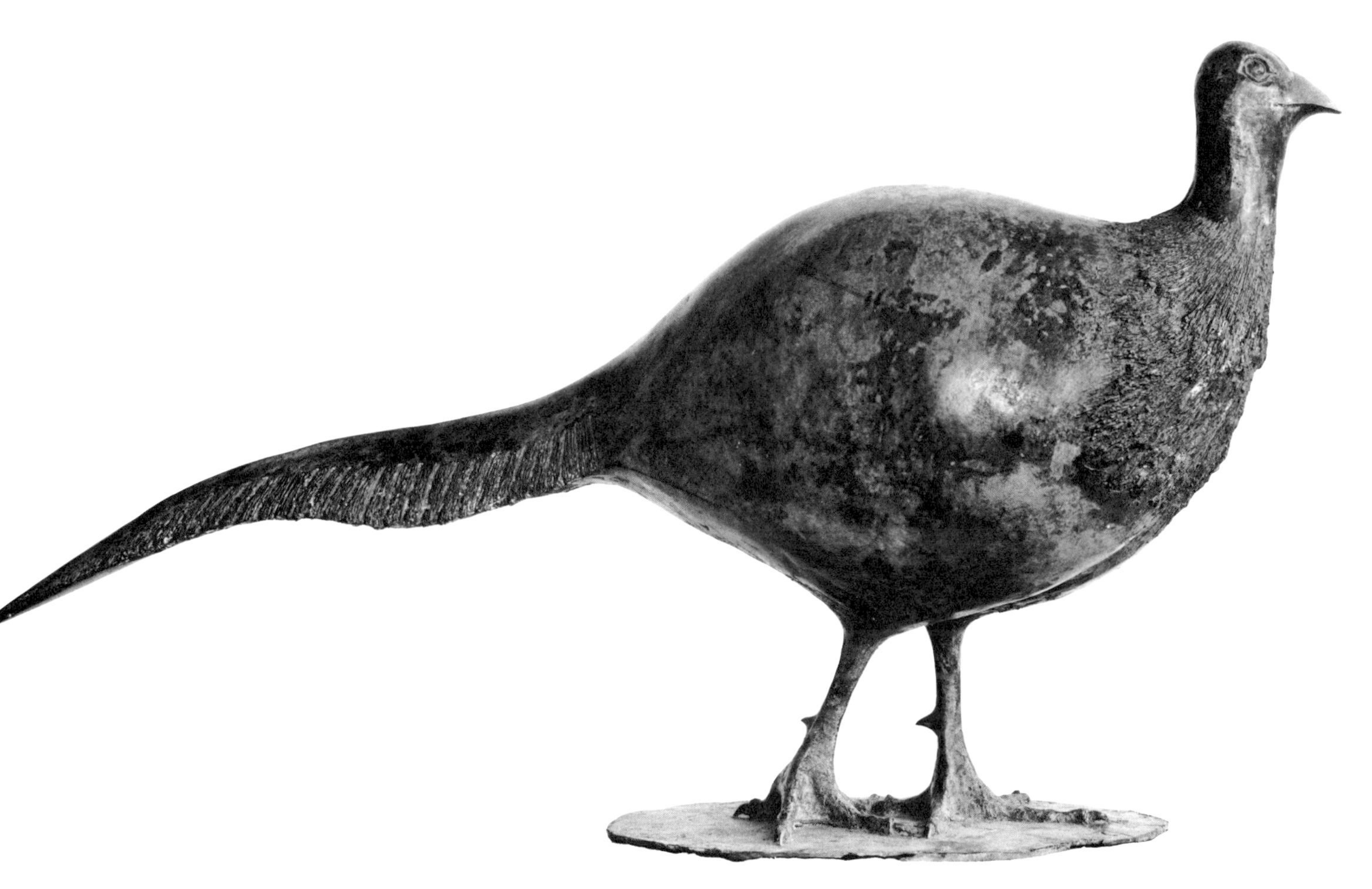

26. *PHEASANT*, 1978/84, Bronze, 19 x 7 x 38

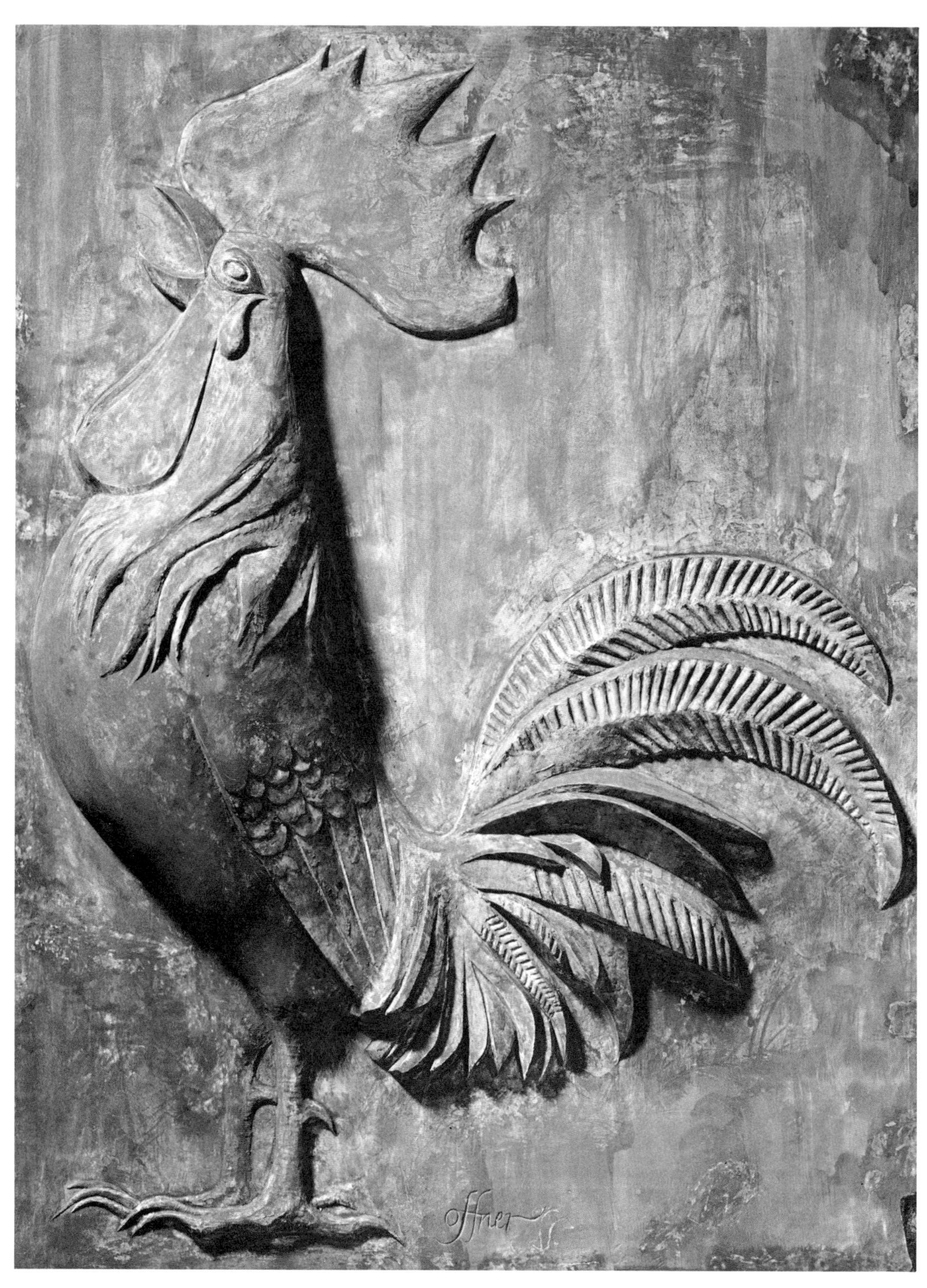

27. *COCKEREL*, 1984, Plaster (relief), 27^7/8 x 20^7/8

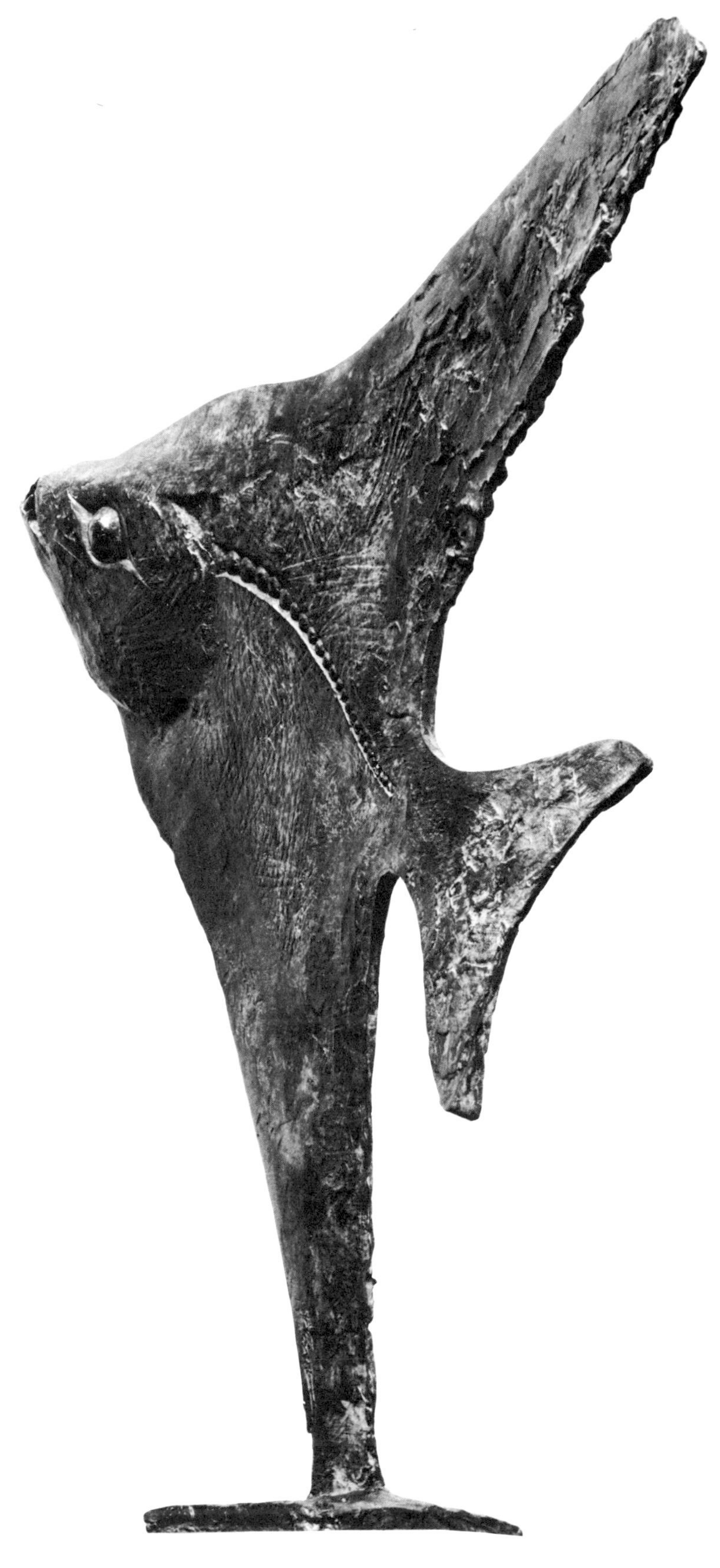

28. Maquette for *ANGEL FISH*, 1984, Bronze, $18^{1}/_{4}$ x $3^{3}/_{4}$ x $17^{3}/_{8}$

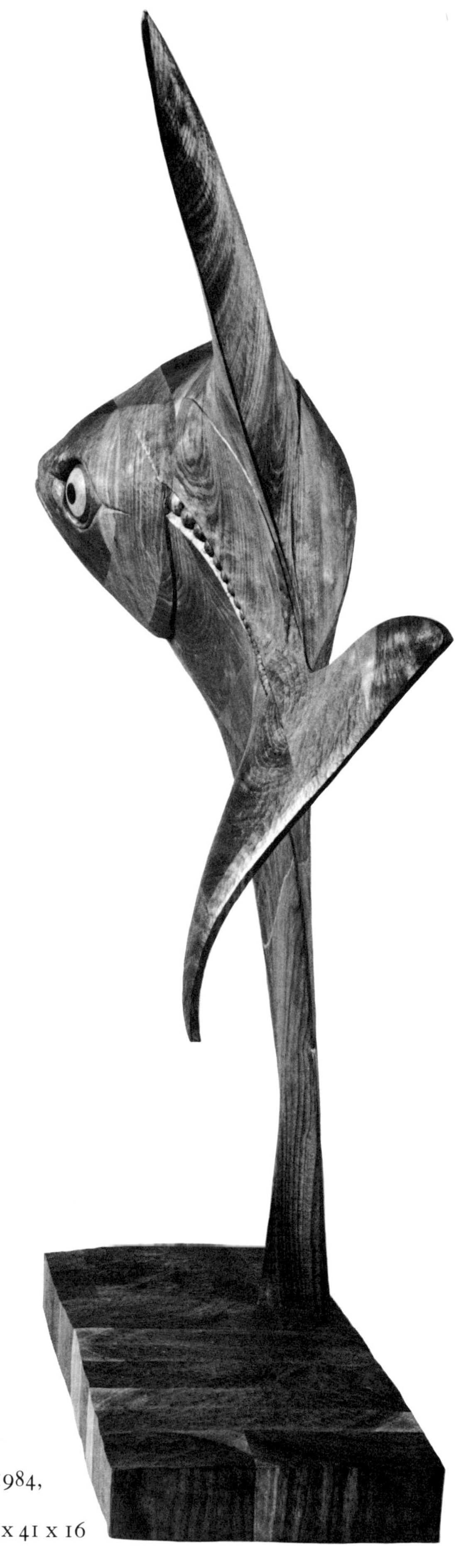

29. *ANGEL FISH*, 1984,

Wood (Cherry), 41 ½ x 41 x 16

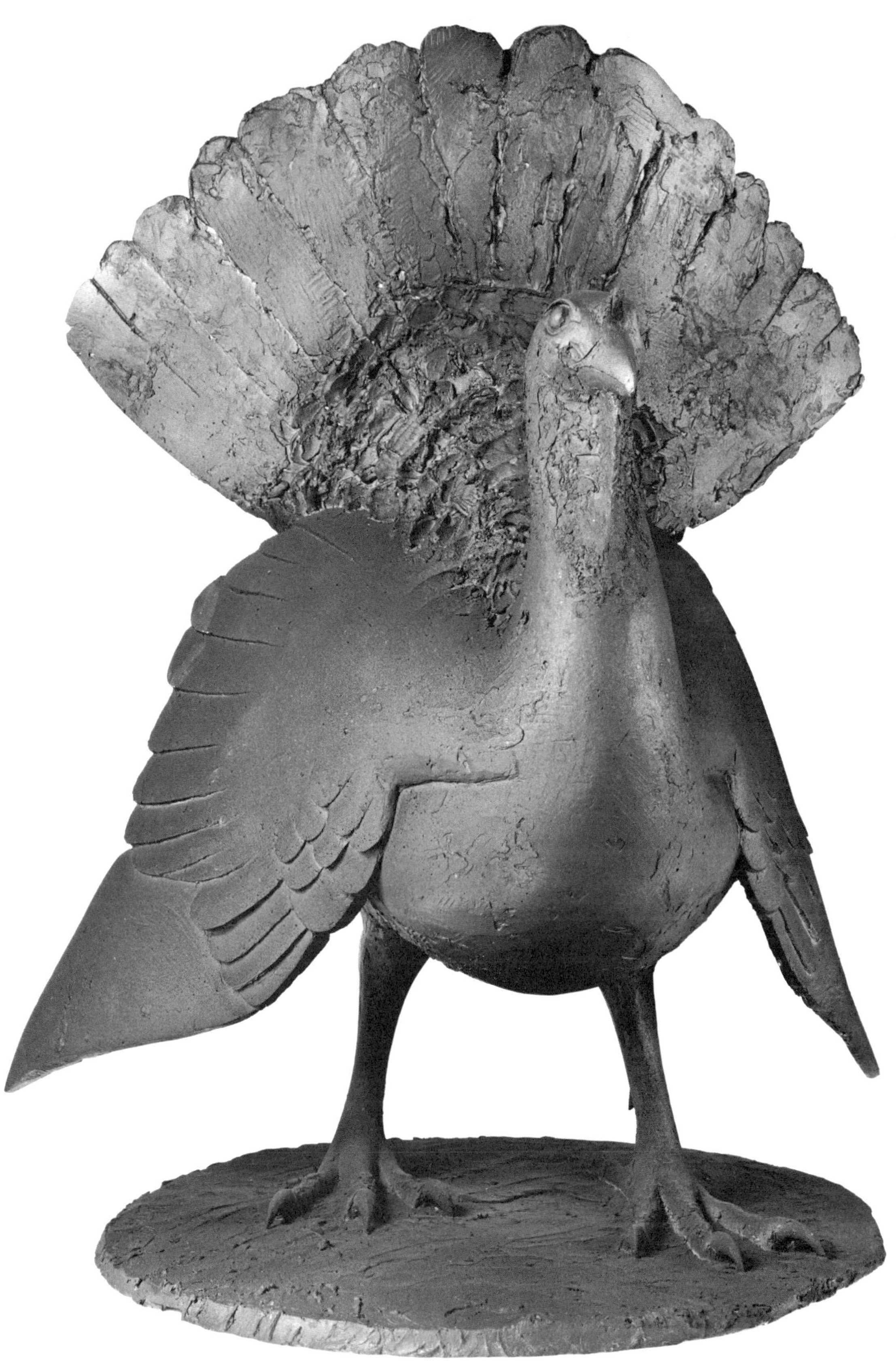

30. *TURKEY*, 1984, Bronze, 32 x 25$\frac{1}{2}$ x 20$\frac{1}{2}$

DESIGNED BY ELLIOT OFFNER

SET IN TYPE AND PRINTED BY

THE STINEHOUR PRESS & THE

MERIDEN GRAVURE COMPANY